Death in the Balance

Death in the Balance

The Debate over Capital Punishment

DONALD D. HOOK

LOTHAR KAHN

Lexington Books

D.C. Heath and Company • Lexington, Massachusetts • Toronto

Library of Congress Cataloging-in-Publication Data

Hook, Donald D., 1928–
Death in the balance : the debate over capital punishment / Donald
D. Hook, Lothar Kahn.
p.   cm.
Bibliography: p.
Includes index.
ISBN 0-669-20905-8 (alk. paper)
ISBN 0-669-20906-6 (pbk.: alk. paper)
1. Capital punishment.   2. Capital punishment—United States.
I. Kahn, Lothar.   II. Title.
HV8694.H66   1989
364.6'6—dc20   89-8206
                                                                    CIP

Published simultaneously in Canada
Printed in the United States of America

The paper used in this publication meets
the minimum requirements of American National Standard
for Information Sciences—Permanence of Paper
for Printed Library Materials, ANSI Z39.48-1984.

Year and number of this printing:

91 92 8 7 6 5 4 3

To my young cousin, Kathryn Hinnant Johnson, M.D., and her
unborn child, murder victims at Bellevue Hospital,
New York City, January 7, 1989.—DDH

Contents

Preface

*You shall fade suddenly like the grass, which in the morning is
green and groweth.*

I N the United States a bitter war is being waged over the proper
way to handle criminals. At the beginning of 1989, the American
public was being told the depressing news that crime was up by 25
to 30 percent in many urban areas and down in none; and that much
of the problem was due to the traffic in and use of drugs. In the 1988
presidential race, the candidate who made the more fervent guarantees that he would not look the other way, that he would get tough
on criminals, and that he would support capital punishment was the
clear victor. In the eyes of many observers, crime was the issue that
gave victory to George Bush.

Who is it that can best ensure the public's safety? Based on only
superficial evidence, the public generally thinks that it is those who
will not stand for crime and who want criminals to get their just
deserts—and if that means taking their lives, so be it. Most people
believe that "pampering" criminals must cease and that such hard-
won penal reforms as parole, furloughs, and probation must be reex-
amined, if not eliminated. They are persuaded that criminals have
inflicted pain and that therefore it is pain they must suffer. Criminals
who have brought about the death of others must pay with their own
lives. People are convinced that if criminals are executed, shady
characters with evil inclinations will think twice before they too violate the lives, the bodies, or the minds, of innocent citizens.

This portrait suggests that the American public is a vindictive,
even bloodthirsty lot. But the evidence shows that, to the contrary,
when these same determinedly retributive citizens serve on a jury or
act in some judicial capacity, they are far more lenient. Despite the
rising crime rate and the mounting number of death sentences that

are asked for and handed down, juries by and large avoid the responsibility of putting people to death. While the inhabitants of death row are getting more numerous, executions remain relatively rare. Whether it be by the old method of hanging or the allegedly humane one of administering lethal injection, juries have been less than eager to end people's lives by their own actions.

There are also opponents of the death penalty who view retribution as sheer immorality and deterrence as a figment of the imagination. They claim—also with little proof—that inflicting the death penalty has contributed nothing to reducing the crime rate. They regard the death penalty as little more than vestigial cruelty, a desperate expression of helplessness in the face of physical insecurity. It is not that they wish to look away after a crime has been committed; they do insist that criminals be prevented from ever transgressing again. Many therefore support incarceration for life without parole.

But the truths of the matter are not all as clear-cut as either side makes them out to be. As a social issue, the death penalty is closely related to two other social issues that have received attention in the news media in the past two decades: abortion and gun control. All three issues raise fundamental questions about life and death, especially the sanctity of life.

It is ironic that relatively little consistency is found among the partisans for and against these issues. To the extent that generalization is possible, many of those who support retaining capital punishment oppose abortion. Many of the strictest retentionists are just as uncompromisingly opposed to gun control. At the same time, opponents of the death penalty tend to support the right to abortion. A related issue, the right to die of the terminally ill who have been vegetating for months and years, is a favorite cause of those who wish to keep criminals alive.

Would it not be logical for the Right, which fights vigorously for the life of a two-week-old fetus, to tolerate the right to life of a twenty-year-old criminal? Would one not expect the Right, which fights so energetically for the life of unborn children, to oppose the uncontrolled sale of handguns?

Would it not be logical for the Left, which fights for the lives of hardened murderers—because they are human, despite all—also to battle for the right of a fetus to develop into a life? Would one not expect opponents of the death penalty to oppose taking the critically sick off life-support systems? At least the Left is consistent in its advocacy of stricter gun control.

In fairness to both positions, it must be said that the issue of abortion deals with the taking of an *innocent* life. In the matter of gun control, other issues are at stake. There is much debate over when a fetus becomes a human being, and advocacy of euthanasia is motivated by the desire to eliminate pain.

If the sanctity of life were the only concern, both sides would have to unite in opposing the death penalty, abortion, and euthanasia and in backing ruthless gun control. But such a plank would receive little support from any of those who invoke the sanctity of life when it suits them. Instead, both sides stand by their long-stated attitudes, one group accusing the other of sentimental idealism, maudlin foolishness, and dreamlike compassion, the other charging its opposition with lack of heart, a tough realism that has little room for compassion, and rampant selfishness.

This standoff is the point where we begin our account. We attempt to present the case for both sides in a balanced, fair way.

Acknowledgments

We wish to express our thanks to attorneys Geoffrey and Susan Kahn for their helpful suggestions in composing chapter 4.

1

The Issues

Read not to contradict and confute, nor to believe and take for granted, nor to find talk and discourse, but to weigh and consider.

— Sir Francis Bacon

CLARENCE DARROW, one of the greatest trial lawyers this country has ever produced, predicted in the 1920s that the death penalty would soon be abolished everywhere. The nearly seventy years that followed have proved him wrong. If abolishing capital punishment is progress toward true humaneness, then the nations of Western Europe, most of which have done away with the death penalty, have come closer to reaching this goal than the United States. For every step Americans have taken toward that goal during the twentieth century, they have also taken a step away from it.

Such a zigzag course probably means that Americans have a genuine uncertainty, based on the variety of their backgrounds, values, and convictions, about the death penalty. Some favor it as necessary and just. Others are equally convinced that it is futile and immoral. Still others are confused about it; they may feel that capital punishment prevents or deters crimes, but they don't want the state to kill a human being in their name. Some believe a heinous crime calls for a heinous punishment; others claim that the preservation of life is the highest value, and that no one has the right to violate it. For opponents of the death penalty, life imprisonment with or without parole is a valid alternative punishment for an individual who has been found guilty of murder, treason, or rape.

People's feelings about capital punishment soar and plunge like mercury in a thermometer depending on the heat of passion aroused by a spate of murders or hijackings or an unusually large number of executions. Most recently, there has been much clamoring for imposing the death penalty for drug-related crimes of a severe nature.

But many other issues seem to influence other people: the finality of death as punishment, the possible execution of innocent persons, the protection of the individual versus the protection of society, the rights of victims as opposed to those of criminals, the difference between a crime of passion and one committed in cold blood, the method of execution, and even the cost factor of life imprisonment.

Religious leaders, students of crime and psychology, and many others have studied the issues surrounding the death penalty and have produced an array of statistics and many arguments of a moral, psychological, and sociological nature. These expert studies do not always influence the average citizen, whose reaction may be mainly emotional. Whereas some opinion polls tell us that three-fourths of the people support the death penalty, others indicate that a little over half the U.S. population favors the death penalty, while the other half favors life imprisonment with or without parole. Given the broad range of expert opinions and people's attitudes based on their religion, social values, and individual experience, this division of opinion within the United States is natural. Moreover, the U.S. Constitution warns against inflicting "cruel and unusual punishment" and says that legal justice is to be meted out fairly and not arbitrarily. Given this, the controversy between opponents of the death penalty and those who wish to retain it is less well drawn than might be hoped for.

The difficulty of finding a clear and uniform basis for imposing the death penalty may be seen in the following cases. In each case, the facts seem to have been weighed carefully; the jury rendered a guilty verdict; and the judge imposed the sentence dutifully. The sentence, however, was not the same in all the cases.

Why? The times during which the various cases were tried were different; political factors were at play; in some cases it was not what the accused had done that was important but who he was—like the character in Albert Camus's novel *The Stranger* who was convicted of a crime less for the crime itself than for his failure to cry at his mother's wake.

Arthur Bishop

On a beautiful spring day in 1988, condemned serial child-killer Arthur Gary Bishop went to his execution at Point of the Mountain, Utah. Eight minutes after two executioners at Utah State Prison injected him with deadly chemicals, he was pronounced dead.

The execution of Arthur Bishop was different in many ways from most of the executions that have taken place since the death penalty was given a new life in the United States in 1976. Bishop was white, while most inmates on death row in U.S. prisons are black. He was sick, and he knew it. He had killed five boys—shooting one, bludgeoning a second, and strangling and drowning the others. Furthermore, he was glad he had been caught because he knew he couldn't control his own sexual behavior. Unlike most killers, he wanted to end his legal appeals after the Utah Supreme Court rejected his arguments against the death penalty.

Bishop had been an Eagle Scout, a Mormon missionary, and a bookkeeper. He became the one hundredth person to be executed in the United States since 1976.

Bishop had brutally killed five times, and he knew that if given a chance, he would kill again. Should he have been executed?

Most Americans answered yes, he should have. He had committed multiple murders and committed them in heinous fashion, thereby giving up his right to live. He had taken life; he must now give a life. Surrendering his own life would provide the ultimate guarantee that he would never murder again. Moreover, they argued, public knowledge that Bishop had paid with his life would deter others from becoming killers.

But others said that killing Bishop served no useful purpose. Although numerous criminals have been executed, the death penalty has never served as a deterrent. It is, moreover, morally contemptible and a violation of the Sixth Commandment, which says, "Thou shalt not kill." Even though Bishop had violated this commandment five times, the state should not follow suit. For the state to kill Bishop was the most "premeditated murder" possible, more than Bishop's own heinous murders, some of which were committed out of fear and anxiety.

Sacco and Vanzetti

Very different in nature was the famous Sacco and Vanzetti case. In this case there may have been a serious miscarriage of justice. But if political considerations did indeed railroad Nicola Sacco, twenty-nine, and Bartolomeo Vanzetti, thirty-two, to their deaths, justice fell victim to these political considerations.

On April 15, 1920, in South Braintree, Massachusetts (a small city not far from Boston), a robbery and murder took place that led to one of the century's most celebrated judicial cases. On that afternoon a paymaster and guard were transporting by foot a $16,000 payroll from a factory office to the plant itself for distribution in precounted small-envelope amounts to the workers. Suddenly, two men armed with pistols—later described as "foreign-looking"—wordlessly accosted and fatally wounded them. Then a car drove up with two other men inside and a third on the running board brandishing a pistol. The murderers heaved the cash box aboard and climbed into the car themselves, and all five drove off at breakneck speed. They then abandoned this car, which had been stolen some six months before, in some woods outside town and left in another that they had stashed nearby.

One day some three weeks later, a garage owner called the police to say that he was sure that the first car was in his shop for repair. By the time the police arrived at the scene, two of the four Italians who had brought the car in had departed on a motorcycle. The remaining two, Sacco and Vanzetti, were seen boarding a streetcar and promptly arrested. Both men were armed and were acting in a suspicious manner.

There had been no shortage of witnesses to the robbery and shooting, but the witnesses disagreed and contradicted each other about the identities of the assailants. Unfortunately for Sacco and Vanzetti, they were the only two men to appear in the lineup, and they were forced to assume banditlike positions. It is not surprising that enough fingers were pointed at them to send them to trial.

The evidence presented against them at the seven-week trial was flimsy and incomplete. There was little agreement among the witnesses; no motive was uncovered; the money was never found; and there was prejudice against "foreigners."

Sacco and Vanzetti swore they had been nowhere near the scene of the crime on April 15. The results of the ballistics tests were controversial. Evidence was introduced that both men were draft dodgers, despite their plea that they were pacifists. The judge even allowed the prosecuting attorney complete leeway in questioning the accused about their anarchistic political beliefs—a matter of no relevance to the crime.

After deliberating less than five hours, the jury returned a verdict of first-degree murder, which carried the death penalty. For six years afterward, motions for a new trial were brought—all were denied. There were appeals for mercy and requests for a pardon, even a posthumous one—and all were denied. Sacco and Vanzetti undertook to exonerate themselves by writing countless letters in broken English. Vanzetti wrote his favorite teacher: "Tank to you from the bottom of my earth for your confidence in my innocence; I am so. I did not splittel a drop of blood, or still a cent in all my life." Sacco wrote some fellow anarchists: "From the deau, cell, we are just informe from the Defense Committee that the governor Fuller has descide to kill us Ag. the 10th."

On that date in 1927, the two men were electrocuted in Charlestown Prison. Ironically, while he was being strapped into the chair, Sacco yelled out in Italian, "Long live anarchy!"

The Sacco and Vanzetti case filled the headlines for months and years afterward. It became the subject of a play, Maxwell Anderson's 1935 *Winterset*, and underscored for death penalty abolitionists the extraordinary dangers of the death penalty. If people could be executed for what they are and not for what they do, then many people would feel vulnerable and unsafe. Much of the evidence was questionable; suppose—just suppose—the two men had been innocent? They could not be recalled into life. The Sacco-Vanzetti case raised numerous questions and gnawed at the conscience of many; equally important, it kept alive the debate on the death penalty.

Leopold and Loeb

The debate was further intensified by an intriguing 1920s murder case, the so-called thrill-killing by two Chicago youths, Nathan Leopold and Richard Loeb. The teenage sons of multimillionaires, the world could have been their oyster, for they were also brilliant young college graduates. Their plan was to commit the perfect crime.

Briefly, they planned a murder and carried it out flawlessly—up to a point. Together they composed a ransom note demanding $10,000, addressed to no one as yet. On May 21, 1924, they went in search of a victim. That's right—they had no particular person in mind! They only knew that it would be unwise to choose somebody who was physically more adroit than they or somebody with whom they had had a previous disagreement. Loeb even suggested that they kill his younger brother; certainly no one would suspect them of such a deed. They rented a car and drove past a private school in their home neighborhood that Loeb himself had once attended. They pinned their attention on a boy who was walking away from the school by himself. It was fourteen-year-old Bobby Franks, a youngster who lived across the street from the Loebs and who had often played tennis with Richard on the Loebs' private court.

It was not hard to entice Bobby into the car. Nathan was driving, and Richard and Bobby got in the back. Two blocks down the street, Richard pulled a heavy cold chisel out from under the seat and clubbed Bobby over the head with it repeatedly. The child died almost immediately, but Richard stuffed old rags into his mouth just to make sure he did not make any loud final noises. He tossed an old horse blanket over the body.

They drove around town for several hours waiting for it to get dark. Then they stripped the body naked, poured acid on the face, and stuffed the corpse into a railroad culvert in an area where Leopold occasionally went to watch swamp birds. Some of Bobby's clothing they buried; the rest they took home and burned. They mailed off the ransom note to Mr. Franks, parked the car in front of Loeb's house, went to bed, and slept peacefully. In the morning they washed the bloodstains off the interior of the automobile and returned it to the rental agency.

The police were led to the murderers indirectly and by stages, through the discovery of a pair of glasses that were lying near the culvert. They turned out to belong to Nathan Leopold. He offered a plausible explanation—he frequently watched birds in the area and must have dropped them on a recent expedition. He and Richard also had an alibi for the night in question—one that soon exploded in their faces. Then separately—inexplicably and without undue pressure—they both spewed forth confessions.

The public wanted their hides. If ever anyone had "earned" the death penalty, it was they. Darrow defended them by pleading them guilty in order to avoid a jury trial, knowing that any jury would hang them. Pleading guilty would entitle them to a hearing on the sentence before a judge. They got life imprisonment.

Few people were happy with this sentence. In fact, the abolitionists seemed to have disappeared from the scene. The Sacco and Vanzetti case was still in the air. If capital punishment had been wrong for the perhaps innocent Sacco and Vanzetti, wasn't it equally wrong for the guilty Leopold and Loeb? Moreover, the social position of the defendants became an issue. Should the ability to hire the best lawyer keep wanton murderers from suffering the death penalty? Was there one system of justice for the poor and another for the rich?

Yet a postscript to the Leopold and Loeb trial might also support a case for life imprisonment as opposed to capital punishment. Both these highly intelligent young men gave much of their time in prison to instructing their fellow inmates in history, mathematics, and foreign languages. They even composed whole textbooks for use in prison. After nine years of incarceration, Richard Loeb was murdered by a fellow convict, possibly after Loeb had made a homosexual advance. Leopold was paroled in 1958 at age fifty-three. He immediately left for the outback of Puerto Rico, where he worked for a pittance at a church-operated hospital. Eventually he earned a master's degree at the University of Puerto Rico, married a woman his own age, and continued to serve humankind until his death from heart trouble in 1971. He felt utter remorse for his part in the killing of Bobby Franks and atoned for it completely.

Julius and Ethel Rosenberg

Only slightly less controversial than the Sacco-Vanzetti and Leopold-Loeb cases was the Rosenberg case. As in the case of the Italian anarchists, the political climate of the time almost certainly played a role. For the Rosenberg case was the first trial to result in the execution of U.S. citizens for conspiracy to commit espionage.

In 1950 the FBI arrested Julius and Ethel Rosenberg for con-

spiring to transmit highly classified information on the atomic bomb
to the Soviet Union. Julius was an electrical engineer by profession
and had worked for the U.S. Signal Corps. Ethel's brother, David
Greenglass, who had worked for the atomic bomb project at Los
Alamos, New Mexico, accused his sister and Julius of having persuaded him to pass on to them and one Harry Gold top-secret data
on atomic weapons. For this crime Julius and Ethel received the
death sentence; Morton Sobell, a codefendant, and Harry Gold received thirty years each; and David Greenglass received fifteen
years. Numerous court appeals and pleas for executive clemency
notwithstanding, the Rosenbergs were electrocuted on June 19,
1953.

Many felt that the Rosenbergs had gotten what they deserved
because they had endangered the security of the United States. Others argued that the information they had handed over to the Soviets
was of less value than touted, and therefore the punishment had not
fit the crime. In short, it became a monstrous controversy.

Caryl Chessman

Seven years later, the death penalty controversy was intensified by
the unique case of Caryl Chessman. After an unprecedented twelve
years on death row, Chessman—after his case had been publicized
as much if not more than any other—was put to death in the gas
chamber.

Chessman never admitted any guilt. He was accused of being
the "Red-Light Bandit," who, flashing a red spotlight on his car, had
driven up to people in their cars while they were parked in a lover's
lane and robbed them and, on at least two occasions, had forced the
women to perform fellatio on him. A number of victims and witnesses asserted that it was Chessman. Despite faulty and even downright inaccurate identification by the victims, Chessman was found
culpable and convicted. Why?

One reason Chessman was suspect was his background. His
whole family had been wracked by illness, accident, and emotional
disorders. Once Caryl had even saved his father's life by pulling his
head out of a gas oven. At the time Caryl had been suffering from
diphtheria. These traumas produced an irascible youngster who had
numerous brushes with the law and spent time in reform school and
later in adult prison for armed robbery. While in jail, Chessman ex-

hibited traits of intelligence and industry despite his disagreeable personality. He advanced his own education through correspondence courses and taught his illiterate fellow convicts how to read; he wrote radio scripts and joined the prison debating team. The prison officials were impressed and approved his transfer to a minimum-security facility. However, he promptly escaped; after being apprehended, he was placed in maximum security.

In 1947 Caryl Chessman was paroled. Only weeks later, he was arrested and charged with the Red-Light Bandit crimes. The prosecuting attorney called him "depraved and vicious"; the jury and judge agreed. He was given the death penalty for kidnapping; to that sentence were added noncapital sentences amounting to life imprisonment as well.

Through appeals, Chessman was able to gain eight stays of execution. When the ninth execution date was fixed, he despaired and said he was lost, that not even he could be expected to have more lives than a cat.

Regardless of what people thought about Chessman the man, many were of the opinion that he had several good reasons to expect another trial. For one, it appeared that the judge had left the jury with the impression that the death penalty was mandatory under California law if a defendant was found guilty—a clear contradiction of the intention of that law.

Caryl Chessman's case became an international cause célèbre. Many believed he had been genuinely rehabilitated. The man had educated himself and written books—one of them, *Cell 2455, Death Row*, had become a best-seller. In his own words: "The long years lived in this crucible called Death Row have carried me beyond bitterness, beyond hate, beyond savage animal violence. Death Row has compelled me to study as I have never studied before, to accept disciplines I would never have accepted otherwise, and to gain a penetrating insight into all phases of this problem of crime that I am determined to translate into worthwhile contributions toward ultimate solution of that problem."

William Henry Furman

One could say that the Chessman case was the last really "big" case involving the death penalty until William Henry Furman, a mildly retarded black man from Georgia, was convicted of killing a man by shooting through a door while carrying out a burglary. But the Furman case was "big" in quite a different way. Although he received the death penalty, Furman's sentence was never carried out because the U.S. Supreme Court made a decision on June 29, 1972, that altered legal matters for years to come. The crux of the decision turned on the phrase "cruel and unusual punishment," a phrase of such importance that we examine it and its implications in more detail in chapter 3. Its effect was to temporarily eliminate the death penalty by voiding federal and state capital punishment laws then operative. But it allowed Congress or state legislatures to enact new death penalty statutes in the future.

Immediately after the *Furman* decision the death penalty seemed well on its way out. But the crime rate rose significantly in the 1970s and 1980s; and whenever the public becomes anxious about its security, in its terror and despair it seeks desperate measures to arrest the trend. Many held that the elimination of the death penalty had been responsible for the increase in murders and in crime in general. Thus the debate continues.

It all makes for interesting and challenging study and debate. The reader is invited to read the chapters that follow and to reach a personal conclusion. If you doubt any of the facts presented, you should investigate further on your own. Law, order, fairness, and compassion must all be seen together. Somehow the rights of individuals and the rights of society must be joined and balanced. The sanctity of an individual life versus the sanctity of society—the problem is to balance that equation. It is not an easy task, as we will see.

2

A Penalty with a Long Past

. . . the ghostly consciousness of wrong.

— Thomas Carlyle

THE year is 1379. The country is England. A young man is being taken from a prison and loaded onto a rickety hurdle. Then he is dragged several hundred yards to a gallows standing alone in an open meadow. He is stood upright and urged forward to his place of execution. The gaping crowd, which has gathered early, cheers wildly. The man disturbed the peace the night before and is about to get his just deserts.

The prisoner catches sight of the gallows. He cries out and resists his captors but is slapped into submission and pushed toward one of the two ladders. He climbs up; the hangman on the ladder next to him slips the rope around his neck. At the top, the rope is fastened around a horizontal beam. The hangman descends his ladder and kicks the prisoner's ladder out from under him. There is a snap, and then a choking sound comes from the condemned man.

The hangman climbs back up, reaches over, and cuts him down. The man's body plops onto the ground. The hangman descends his ladder, produces a sharp knife, lifts the man's tunic, and deftly disembowels him on the spot. As his entrails spill out, they are gathered up and tossed into a fire. With an ax the executioner severs the man's head from his body.

The man appears to die only after his head is lopped off. But the torso twitches for a full minute thereafter. The executioner slices up the corpse into four quarters and spears each onto a stob stuck into the ground.

The cheers of the crowd drown out the sounds of two or three people retching.

Over a thousand men were executed like this in England in 1379, many for the most trivial of crimes.

The year is 1979, and the country the United States. A flailing man is being pulled by several guards down the hall from his room on death row to a small, immaculately clean chamber. In the center of the chamber is a wooden chair, wired and ready. The man is strapped in, fitted with a metal cap, and hooded. Heavy-duty wires leading out of a box on the wall are snapped onto the cap and onto electrodes attached to the condemned man's legs and arms. Two hooded executioners stand prepared to pull the switch. And then it is done. The prisoner's body is jolted as the current surges through it; smoke rises from the arms, legs, and head of the man. The body, first in convulsion, goes limp. Shortly thereafter, the man is officially pronounced dead.

This man was one of only two persons executed in 1979. Both were murderers.

Is this progress? The prisoner in medieval England was executed shortly after his trial. His execution was a source of merrymaking. His execution was witnessed by many and perhaps served as a warning to the crowd. The prisoner in modern America died after years of legal appeals, in the near privacy of the execution site. Only a few official observers watched the murderer "pay his debt to society." The event served as a direct warning only to these persons, and it may have served indirectly as a deterrent to the millions who read sanitized accounts of it in the newspapers.

Clearly, in the six hundred years that separate the two executions, the methods of putting criminals to death have improved greatly. Today's are less cruel. They show less evidence of revenge and more respect for the dignity of the human being. They appear to be faster, though the criminal of today has had death and doubt staring at him for several painful years.

An execution is nonetheless a killing. No one has returned afterward to report on when he or she lost consciousness, what mode of killing hurts more, or which hurts less. Nor have any of those executed come back to say whether the one method or the other would have deterred them from committing the crime for which they atoned with their life.

Over the centuries, the reduction in the number of capital offenses from literally hundreds to two or three in most countries and to none in others is impressive. Equally important has been the decrease in the arbitrariness by which crimes are selected for capital punishment, especially in the capriciousness of finding one person guilty of a capital offense and finding another innocent of the same crime. From the earliest days down to the present, the treatment of criminals has varied with their social position. In ancient Rome, a freeman who had killed another freeman was treated more leniently than a freeman who had killed a slave and certainly more leniently than a slave who had killed anyone else. Kings, magistrates, and— later—juries treated upper-class criminals with greater consideration and exempted them from the death penalty more readily than persons from the anonymous masses. Even a cursory review of the history of capital punishment lends support to the contention that in the twentieth century the death penalty is still reserved mostly for the poor and the deprived.

But especially in the United States, some claim that the criminal justice system has become excessively preoccupied with the rights of capital offenders and is insufficiently concerned with the memory of, the damage done to, and the lost potential of heinously murdered victims and their families. This is an irrelevant concern, say others— mostly opponents of the death penalty—as they examine the sweep of history. For them the history of capital punishment reveals that a society that kills is inhuman, however evil and despicable its victims.

Let us see where we have come from in order to determine where we are and may still be going.

A Life for a Life and a Life for a Dime

The Ancient Codes

The sentence of death may have existed even before society was organized on a tribal basis—certainly long before there were courts, tribunals, and manpower to carry out their verdicts. For example, in early societies a father might condemn a member of his family to death if he felt that he or she had incurred the wrath of the gods. If a brother or sister committed incest, he or she would be put to death by other members of the clan seeking to protect themselves. Then the gods had to be pacified for having witnessed the misdeeds of the guilty.

As human society became organized into larger social units, legal codes of one kind or another became necessary. The codes of primitive peoples were extremely harsh, and they dispensed death freely for a vast number of public and private violations. The Sumerian law codes (the laws of Eshunna) and the codes of Li K'nei in China all attest to the severity with which infringements of laws were dealt. To this day some societies in South America and West Africa into which modern thinking has made few inroads retain laws that have more in common with those of early societies than with those of Europe and the United States.

In ancient Greece, the Athenian lawgiver Draco prescribed death for nearly any misdeed. We know about his Draconian Code (c. 621 B.C.) through the writings of Plutarch, who wrote in his *Lives* in his life of Solon: "One penalty was assigned to almost all transgressions, namely death, so that even those convicted of idleness were put to death and those who stole salt or fruit received the same punishment as those who committed sacrilege or murder. Therefore Demades, in later times, made a hit when he said that Draco's laws were written not with ink but blood. And Draco himself, they say, being asked why he made death the penalty for most offenses, replied that in his opinion the lesser ones deserved it, and for the greater ones no heavier penalty could be found." The phrase *Draconian measure* has thus come to mean an extreme in cruel measures.

Although the penalty was uniformly death, Draco's code did have two clear advantages. First, it codified law by writing the laws down, thereby preventing arbitrariness. Second, it is believed that Draco was the first to distinguish between intentional murder and other kinds.

The code was so severe that it was not enforceable for long. Solon (c. 640–559 B.C.), another Athenian statesman and lawgiver, drafted a new code that greatly reduced the number of offenses that were punishable by death. It would not have occurred to Solon to remove the death penalty for murder, treason, or similar severe crimes. So began a pattern of severity of punishment, followed by mildness, and then by severity again—a pattern that seems to have persisted into our own time.

The older codes of Hammurabi and Moses were less stringent than Draco's but stricter than Solon's. Many of Hammurabi's laws, applicable in Babylonia around 1750 B.C., were based on the idea of equal retaliation. This means that if person A knocks out the eyes of person B, A's own eyes are to be removed. The same applies to a tooth knocked out or any other bodily organ destroyed.

The Mosaic laws of several centuries later retained the idea of equal retaliation; that is, revenge was permitted only in relation and only in proportion to an offense. Thus the notion stated in Exodus 21:23–25 "life for life, eye for eye, tooth for tooth, hand for hand, foot for foot, burning for burning, wound for wound, stripe for stripe" is anchored in older legislation. The idea of "an eye for an eye and a tooth for a tooth" was interpreted less as a law or injunction than as a limitation on the penalty that could be imposed.

Certainly, the evidence for how much the ancient Hebrews imposed the death penalty is neither definitive nor clear in the Old Testament. The Old Testament preached the sanctity of human life. The Sixth Commandment, "Thou shalt not kill," has been seen as a command not only to the individual not to kill, but also to the state or society not to kill either. In Genesis 4:15, after Cain murders Abel, God puts a mark on Cain to protect him from those who would avenge Abel's death. (Further on, God is quoted as saying, "As I live . . . I have no pleasure in the death of the wicked, but that the wicked shall live.") On the other hand, in Genesis 9:6: "Who sheddeth man's blood shall his blood be shed."

Though these statements are contradictory, some offenses were certainly judged as more harmful than others. Among those requiring the ultimate punishment were the worship of alien gods and false prophecy. Capital crimes of a nonreligious nature were murder, treason, and—more unusual—disobedience to a parent and a bride's keeping from her spouse-to-be the fact that she was not a virgin. Yet regardless of the letter of the law, the authorities were sufficiently mindful of the commandment not to kill that they did not usually enforce the law where the death penalty was called for.

The Bible's statements on the subject of capital punishment are important, of course, because quotations from it are used both in support of and in opposition to the death penalty. In fact, the English law code (which was applied in America in colonial days) cited a biblical passage for every crime deserving of major punishment.

The New Testament is also cited in the death penalty controversy. It is impossible to ignore Jesus's words that he has not come
to abolish the law but to fulfill it—and the existing law at the time
provided for the death penalty in given situations. Jesus's endorse-
ment appears more specific when he states, "Whosoever shall kill
shall be in danger of the judgment." Although "the judgment" is not
identified as the death penalty, such an interpretation can be read
into the declaration.

But there is also the other side. It is often said that the New
Testament, with its emphasis on love, compassion, repentance, and
redemption, is on the whole opposed to the death penalty, regardless
of what individual quotations taken out of context might suggest.
And when Jesus was asked to comment on a man's misdeeds, he was
emphatic: "He that is without sin among you, let him first cast a
stone." Proponents of the death penalty may quote Paul at this point:
"All who take the sword will perish by the sword."

Whatever the evidence, some students of the question put partial
blame for the survival of capital punishment on the Bible. They find
it significant that in the West, death has been a frequent penalty for
crime in times and places where the principles of the Bible constituted the moral force for both individual and government action.

Others place considerable blame on the Roman Catholic Church,
the oldest continuous branch of Christendom in the West and the
one with the greatest influence. Except for statements by Pope
Leo I in the fifth century and by Nicholas I in the ninth dissociating
the Church from violence, the Church has made no official pro-
nouncements on the question—that is, through encyclicals. Its general position today seems to be that imposing the death penalty for
extraordinary crimes is not morally objectionable. Capital punishment is seen as an atonement for the injustice the criminal has per-
petrated against the unity of order. (As one priest put it, "We need
a sense of justice in this world.")

Roman Law

Roman law was definitely more cruel than the laws of the late Greek,
Hebrew, and early Christian periods. In Rome at about 500 B.C.,
vestal virgins were to be burned alive if they violated their vows of
chastity. According to the Law of the Twelve Tables, other curious

offenses that called for the death penalty were removing crops, starting fires, stealing (by a slave), bearing false witness, libeling, and disturbing the peace at night.

Like earlier ancient law codes, the Twelve Tables were based on the idea of equal retaliation (or *lex talionis*), with some peculiar notions of the relationship of the offense to the manner of execution added. Persons found guilty of treason were beheaded; those convicted of perjury were hurled off the Tarpeian rock; an intentional killing resulted in the culprit's being scourged and drowned. A thief was surrendered to his victim, who was free to put the thief to death. Stealing crops at night was punishable by crucifixion and arson, by scourging, and then by being burned alive. One thousand years after Draco's code, the Twelve Tables showed only a small advance in the level of civilization—it contained only a slight reduction in the number of crimes considered capital offenses. Yet by specifying offenses and punishments in writing, the Twelve Tables did curtail the arbitrary power of the magistrates, the wealthy, and the influential.[1]

Toward Greater Humanity

In the later Roman Republic and the early Roman Empire, legislation—as well as the application of laws—became more humane. The number of capital crimes decreased. Theft, embezzlement, sacrilege, and electoral bribery were among those deleted from the death list. For the remaining crimes, practice often permitted the criminal to survive: even after conviction, a citizen was often allowed to remain at liberty long enough to flee into exile, a fate obviously preferable to death. For many crimes, a fine or a retaliatory payment replaced capital punishment. As Roman culture became more refined and its legal system became well-developed, the death penalty increasingly fell out of favor, and the number of executions diminished markedly in comparison with earlier years.[2]

But movement toward greater forbearance and humaneness never proceeds in a straight line. After this decline in the death penalty, it enjoyed a rebirth in the centuries of the Empire. The number of capital offenses was increased once more, as was the cruelty in carrying out executions.

During the thousand years that followed the end of the Roman Empire, some significant cultural achievements were made; but a more lenient attitude about putting people to death was not among them.

The criminal code of the Holy Roman Empire (1532), known as *Constitutio Criminalis Carolina*, contained a catalog of crimes and punishments that was among the worst in Western history. For crimes such as sorcery, arson, counterfeiting, and assorted sexual aberrations, the code called for burning at the stake. Murderers could be beheaded, horse-dragged, or broken on the wheel, depending on the nature of their crime. Serious offenses against king or state—notably treason—were punishable by dismemberment. More "ordinary" crimes, including robbery, rape, and serious brawling, called for beheading. Hanging was the common form of execution. If a judge found mitigating circumstances in a crime, he was authorized to exile the criminal to a nearby state, although often the criminal's eyes were gouged out or he was flogged before he was exiled. For the crime of blasphemy, the judge was bound to order either the death penalty or mutilation. If a woman committed a major crime, she was drowned; if she was found guilty of repeated child-killing, she was buried alive.[3]

This code remained in effect in Austria, Prussia, and other German states until the late eighteenth century. In France the laws were only slightly less harsh, until the French Revolution ushered in a new era. Capital punishment prevailed for numerous crimes against the individual, the state, and property. Almost until the close of the 1700s, the modes of execution were, in the order of use: hanging, beheading, burning at the stake, and breaking on the wheel. Death sentences were frequent since confessions for crimes—real or imagined—could be obtained through torture. Not infrequently, an individual would opt for a quick death in preference to being subjected to prolonged bodily agony at the hands of skilled torturers.

In England, fifty-five crimes were punishable by hanging or worse, which earned the legal code in effect the label of "the Bloody Code." In every country and era where the death penalty has been used, murder, rape, and treason have been the prime offenses. But up to the Victorian era, the Bloody Code also included heresy, vagrancy, and witchcraft. As late as the beginning of the eighteenth century, the number of criminals put to death annually in England was estimated at between seven hundred and eight hundred.

Leon Radzinowicz, in his *History of English Criminal Law*, provided a description of the early nineteenth-century British landscape: it is, he says, dotted with instruments of death. Gallows and gibbets were such common objects that in early guidebooks for travelers they were used as landmarks: "By the Gallows and Three Windmills enter the suburbs of York. . . . You pass through Hare Street . . . and at 13'4 part for Epping Forest, with the gallows on the left. . . . You pass Penmeris Hall, and at 250'4 Hildraught Mill, both on the left, and ascend a small hill with a gibbet on the right. . . . You leave Frampton, Wilberton and Sherbeck, all on the right, and by a gibbet on the left, over a stone bridge."[4] Even in the early nineteenth century, the age of romantic sensibility, when women swooned at the slightest provocation and bearded men shed happy tears in each other's arms, victims were hanged singly or in batches of up to twenty. Frequently, the prisoners were drunk, and the executioner too: "This day Will Summers and Tipping were executed here for housebreaking. At the tree, the hangman was intoxicated with liquor, and supposing that there were three for execution, was going to put one of the ropes round the parson's neck, as he stood in the cart, and was with much difficulty prevented by the gaoler from so doing."[5] Onlookers frequently became rowdy, even hysterical, so that the hangman sometimes became thoroughly unnerved and botched the job. This meant that people occasionally had to be hanged more than once. All too often a holiday mood accompanied public executions. Until well into the nineteenth century, hangings were occasions for bawdy merrymaking and widespread public drinking.

While isolated voices of concern were raised, no outcry against capital punishment was heard in England such as was heard in France. There Voltaire, the personification of the Enlightenment, championed the legal reforms advocated by Cesare Beccaria. Voltaire had put his genius to work rehabilitating three men of his time—all of whom had been tortured and then executed out of nothing more than sheer religious intolerance. He made their deaths meaningful by challenging the authorities who had put them to death.

New Views of Punishment

Cesare Beccaria ranks as a titan among those who fought against capital punishment and for a new way of approaching crime. An eighteenth-century Italian criminologist, economist, and jurist who held high office in the government of Austria, Beccaria was both a product of the Enlightenment and one of its chief contributors. Beccaria wanted human pain to be reduced by lessening the incidence of crime—in fact, by preventing it—but he also sought to lower the suffering of criminals by inflicting only those penalties that were sufficient for prevention. Like Voltaire, whom he influenced, he held that criminals should be punished not for vengeance but for the purpose of deterring future crimes. Deterrence did not require capital punishment, nor certainly the tortures that preceded it.

Early on in his treatise, *Essay on Crimes and Punishments*, Beccaria advocated abolition of the death penalty. But he did justify it in one case. When a person (even if deprived of liberty) has connections and power such as would endanger the security of a nation—for example, if his or her existence "could produce a dangerous revolution"—Beccaria thought there may be no choice but the death penalty. Yet on the whole, he believed that in an enlightened commercial society rather than in a religiously oriented one crimes would be fewer and less violent and punishments could be markedly reduced. He saw the death penalty as merely a temporary deterrent, for public executions made only a momentary impression.[6]

Paradoxically, one of the most fervent followers of Beccaria's doctrines was Maximilien Robespierre. Early in the French Revolution, Robespierre stood up during the debates of the French National Assembly to denounce torture and the death penalty. Yet only two or three years later, after he had come to power, the same Robespierre affixed his powerful name to hundreds of death sentences for "enemies of the Revolution" in a period that has come to be known as the Reign of Terror. As so often in years before and after, a vast gulf existed between theory and practice regarding capital punishment. In dubious fairness to Robespierre, it should be stated that those he condemned were executed by means of the recently invented guillotine, a device that was believed to be a humane advance in methods of doing away with people.

3

Toward Abolition of the Death Penalty

> Indeed, history is nothing more than a tableau of crimes and misfortunes.
>
> — Voltaire

> None are all evil.
>
> — Byron

From Colonial Times to *Furman*

The imposition of capital punishment in the American colonies followed the model of the British homeland, where around fifty-five crimes were still punishable by death. Heresy, vagrancy, and witchcraft could end a life as readily as murder, rape, and treason. Hanging remained the preferred mode of execution, although other methods were also employed. In England, the number of criminals put to death each year continued at over seven hundred. (The number of death sentences handed down was far greater, but legal authorities were often ahead of the laws they were sworn to uphold: Rather than dispatch an accused to his or her death for a minor infraction, a magistrate usually found him not guilty, and a good whipping took the place of the hangman's noose.) Curiously, the citizenry seemed more bloodthirsty than the judges. In 1807, over forty thousand English men, women, and children congregated to cheer at a hanging. The excitement reached such a peak that several dozen people were trampled to death.

The famous witchcraft trials at Salem, Massachusetts, in 1692 showed the colonies' affinity for the British homeland. There, nineteen persons were hanged for witchcraft, and one was pressed to death. Nor was Salem the only city afflicted by execution mania; as the frontier moved slowly westward, impatience with "legal ways" and "justice" and the absence of legal personnel led to many a quick hanging on little more grounds than suspicion and often in the most arbitrary fashion. From the hasty justice of this still-primitive frontier world, it was but one step to summary punishments carried out by self-appointed groups or mobs without any trial by law. When suspicion focused on a black person, capital punishment approached plain bloodthirstiness in its most extreme and irresponsible form: lynching.

The very origin of the word *lynch* reveals uncomfortable truths. Some trace the word back to James Fitz-Steven Lynch, the fifteenth-century mayor of an Irish town who in 1493 executed his own son for murder. Others trace it back to a British sailor named Lynch who did away with pirates without process of law. But most theorists trace it back to the American Revolutionary soldier and zealous patriot, Charles Lynch of Virginia, who ordered Tories to be flogged. The idea that it derives from Lynch's Creek in South Carolina is no more consoling, for that was said to be the meeting place of the Regulators, self-appointed administrators of criminal justice. The latest dictionaries favor its origin in a certain Captain W. Lynch (1742–1820), member of a vigilance committee in Pittsylvania, Virginia, around 1780.

The very harsh attitudes about capital punishment in the home country were thus exported to the colonies. The English Penal Code served as the basis for legal proceedings in the colonies. Unlike the law in force at home, it enumerated fourteen offenses calling for the death penalty, although application of the code differed in the various colonies.

In the Puritan Massachusetts Bay Colony, for example, relatively many crimes were seen as serious enough to justify executions. These included the usual crimes of rape, statutory rape, kidnapping, murder, rebellion, adultery, and buggery. But reflecting the colony's heavily religious cultural emphasis, capital crimes also included idolatry, witchcraft, and blasphemy. For such crimes a quotation from the Bible was usually appended in order to justify the ultimate punishment.

While Puritan Massachusetts was harsh in prescribing capital punishment, Quaker-influenced South Jersey, in its Royal Charter (1646), allowed no capital punishment for any crime. Similarly, William Penn's Frame of Government in 1682 sharply restricted capital punishment in Pennsylvania to treason and murder. But the South Jersey and Pennsylvania codes were the exception; the other colonies by and large followed the English Penal Code.

Executions Stop

Just as early opposition to capital punishment in Europe is associated with Cesare Beccaria, in the United States it is linked with Benjamin Rush (1745–1813), a signer of the Declaration of Independence. As early as the 1780s Rush publicly attacked killing by society. He advocated a penal reform that succeeded in gaining the support of Benjamin Franklin. Its points included not only doing away with the death penalty but also establishing a House of Reform, a prison in which criminals would remain until they had learned to change their antisocial behavior. In several of his pamphlets, he questioned the support given by the Bible to capital punishment. On deterrence, he took the extreme view that the threat of hanging not only did not deter crime but might possibly increase it. He was convinced that the state has no right to execute its citizens.[1]

Rush, a physician and an early psychiatrist, also advocated more humane treatment for the mentally ill. For him, crime was a disease for which appropriate remedies should be found. Laws should not specify the punishment to be accorded; rather, sentences should be calibrated to the temper of individual criminals or to the evidence they show of reshaping their lives.

Rush's ideas of individualized treatment were expensive and could not be implemented. However, the penitentiary—a place in which a criminal could show signs of penitence—did come into being. It was a far cry in practice from what Rush had envisaged in theory, but it was nonetheless a creditable substitute for the indiscriminate use (as was then customary in England) of the death penalty. Lives were to be rearranged by means of bodily pain, labor, watchfulness, solitude, and silence rather than terminated on the gallows.[2]

This Renaissance man with an Enlightenment outlook was convinced that the state exceeded its powers when it killed one of its citizens. Rush did not convert Ben Franklin to abolitionism, but he did secure the support of other leading Pennsylvania citizens. It was in part due to his influence that in 1794 Pennsylvania reinstituted a reform of 1682 that did away with capital punishment for all crimes except first-degree murder.

In the wake of Rush's efforts, societies advocating abolition sprang up in several states and territories. Michigan (then still a territory) actually abolished capital punishment except for treason. Other states followed suit, only quickly to reinstate it; apparently, many segments of the voting public felt insecure in its absence, and legislators responded to their concern. However, northern states sharply reduced the number of applicable offenses, usually retaining only murder, treason, and sometimes rape, even after they had reinstated the executioner. (Southern states lagged far behind.) Increasingly, states adopted a distinction between first- and second-degree murder and even between intentional and premeditated murder, the latter referring to the cold planning of a heinous deed.

While most likely the majority of the American people never felt secure without the death penalty as a "deterrent," more thoughtful and better-educated segments often totally rejected the notion of capital punishment. Generally, abolitionist sentiment increased during periods of reform and decreased when there was a reaction to change and a desire to stand pat and stabilize. Opinions on the death penalty also varied from region to region; the deep South by and large clung to capital punishment, while the Mid- and North Atlantic states assumed the vanguard of abolitionism. In these latter states abolitionist societies took a firm hold at midcentury, especially the American Society for the Abolition of Capital Punishment. In 1852 Rhode Island took the lead by eliminating the death penalty, followed soon after by the usually progressive Wisconsin. Nearly all the states markedly reduced the number of capital offenses, generally retaining hanging or alternative methods of execution as punishment for first-degree murder and treason.

The extent to which some states vacillated, moving with events and changing sentiment, is illustrated by the case of Maine. Maine abolished the death penalty after the Civil War, only to reverse itself very shortly thereafter. Less than two decades later, in 1887, Maine reversed itself still again and removed the death penalty from its statutes.

In the first two decades of the twentieth century the abolitionist movement seemed triumphant. Nine states did away with capital punishment. But then, as so often before, the tide turned quickly, and within four years five of these states had reinstated it. During Prohibition interest in the question waned. In the four decades that followed, no other state outlawed capital punishment. Six states and one territory (Puerto Rico) remained with no death penalty in their statutes.

Historians of capital punishment report that there was renewed progress during the period between 1955 and 1972. Yet this progress was small and hesitant. Alaska and Hawaii—still territories—outlawed it in 1957, and for a while it looked as though Delaware would be added to the abolitionist camp. Discarded in 1957, capital punishment made a full comeback there in 1961. During the heady 1960s, however, three other states joined Alaska and Hawaii and relinquished the death penalty, and others reduced the number of crimes for which the criminal would be taken to the gas chamber.

By 1967 the debate surrounding capital punishment had shifted from philosophical, moral, and human grounds to more purely legal grounds. In optimism generated by social changes in the 1960s, abolitionist societies sued Florida and California—the sunny states, with the most criminals on death row—on constitutional grounds. The U.S. Supreme Court was asked to decide whether the death penalty did not violate the "cruel and unusual punishment" provisions of the Constitution (the Eighth Amendment). The suits were sufficient to persuade the Court to stay all executions until it could rule. A lengthy waiting period followed, during which there was an implied understanding that the Court would decide the constitutionality of the death penalty. For an entire decade (until 1977, when a world-weary Gary Gilmore virtually demanded to be executed), the United States went without a single execution.

The decision that shaped the future of capital punishment was *Furman v. Georgia* in 1972. In what was hailed as a landmark decision, the Court ruled—by a five-to-four decision, but with nine separate opinions—that the death penalty did constitute cruel and unusual punishment and that it had often been arbitrarily imposed.

Generally speaking, the liberal members of the Court held that the death penalty was invalid regardless of the severity of the crime; they were not deterred by the fact that the Eighth Amendment had originally been directed against torture rather than against the death penalty. For the two abolitionist justices of the Court, the widened interpretation of the Constitution that had already been made possible by such concepts as "due process," "cruel and unusual punishment," and "equal protection" permits adaptations to each new age: "A penalty that was permissible at one time . . . is not necessarily permissible today."

At the other end of the spectrum, the conservative justices of the Court—often called constructionists—held that both the Fifth and the Fourteenth amendments clearly and unmistakably acknowledge the death penalty. Regardless of the "cruel and unusual punishment" clause, they argued, the wording and the intent of the Constitution make the death penalty constitutional.

The third group of justices of the Furman case avoided any interpretation broader than that relating to the cases before them. They found that sentences and executions were often "arbitrary" and "capricious" and hence unconstitutional. They claimed that, because the death penalty had been imposed rarely and capriciously, executions in the United States did constitute cruel and unusual punishment.[3] One justice held that being "rare and arbitrary" meant that the death penalty was able to perform a deterrent function.

The Court's ruling basically had to do with standards for selecting men and women to be executed. State legislatures were therefore quick to tighten up their laws to have them conform to the ruling. The decision prevented carrying out the death penalty in *Furman* and in other decisions for the time being, but it did not provide a final decision regarding the general validity of capital punishment. The effect was to call a halt to all executions through 1976.

As crime statistics in the United States reached increasingly alarming proportions, especially in urban areas, the public demand for executions became noisier. Support for capital punishment became popular again. Several states that had previously barred the death penalty restored it: Oregon in 1978, New Mexico and Massachusetts the following year, and Ohio in 1981. The attempt on President Ronald Reagan's life in 1981 led to further loud clamoring for the death penalty. (Oddly, the cry for outlawing the sale of guns was more subdued, and state legislatures were unable to pass legislation against their purchase.)

In 1981 then–associate justice of the Supreme Court William H. Rehnquist asked the Court to change its procedures so that the death penalty might be imposed more quickly by states. He deplored the stalemate that allowed sentences of death but made executions so rare. He complained that "the existence of the death penalty in this country is a virtual illusion."[4] His remarks produced no changes.

After *Furman*

Although the period following the *Furman* decision was profoundly disappointing to abolitionists in the United States, the historical trend toward eliminating the death penalty continued in other industrialized nations. Portugal outlawed it in 1977; Norway, Nicaragua, and tiny Luxembourg did so the following year. France removed her famed guillotine in 1981; the Netherlands abolished capital punishment in 1982, and Australia in 1985. Nine other nations reduced the number of capital offenses to only "exceptional" crimes, mostly those punishable by military law or during wartime. Among the countries that retain capital punishment are those, like Belgium, that have not had an execution in forty years. Several countries, such as Brazil and Spain, have abolished, reinstated, and reabolished the death penalty over the past eighty years, like Maine did in this country.

In spite of the essentially staggered worldwide trends regarding capital punishment and the surprise setback in recent U.S. history, legally sanctioned violence by the state has declined as societies have evolved. Cultural evolution on the whole has resulted in a tendency to lessen the severity of penalties (although it does not, of course, proceed in a straight line).

Besides cultural evolution, social and political evolution has also contributed to this tendency. Indeed, the sociopolitical climates of nations and their various legal institutions play a powerful role. In the United States—with its federal judiciary, its unique (though not always happy) method of choosing justices for the Supreme Court, and its powerful litigious social pressure groups—sociopolitical forces have also played a vital role, despite the present, transient direction.

The 1988 U.S. presidential election, which catapulted George Bush into the White House, ensured that there will be a conservative majority on the Supreme Court for a long time to come. President Bush, like President Reagan before him, supports retaining the death penalty. Because as many as three justices are likely to be replaced by him in the next four years, the likelihood of abolishing the death penalty in the next decade is slight.

4

What Does the Law Have to Say?

Justice is a constant and perpetual desire to grant each man his due.
— Justinian, *Institutiones*

IN October 1983 the U.S. Supreme Court, in one of its dramatic late-night decisions, turned down the appeal of the convicted Texas killer James Autry. The vote was close—five to four. The following night, Texas officials were preparing to give Autry a fatal injection when new word came from Washington: Justice Byron White, who was a Kennedy appointee but is regarded as a judicial conservative, had stayed the execution with all of twenty-four minutes to go. Autry's attorneys had received a last-minute inspiration: the death penalty as applied in Autry's case might not be in proportion to the punishments for other crimes in Texas. (Proportionality refers to the comparison of a death sentence in the case before the court with penalties imposed in similar cases.)

Since the Supreme Court was then considering the issue of proportionality in a California case, the stay was quickly granted. Then it was quickly shown that *Autry* exhibited no irregularity in proportionality. Three months later, the Court ruled that proportionality was not even needed. Another appeal by Autry's persistent attorneys failed. He was executed two months later.

The *Autry* case illustrates the rank confusion that existed throughout both higher and lower courts. The hope that the Supreme Court could provide umbrella decisions under which state courts could find ready cover and reduce the number of appeals proved unfounded.

Cases like *Autry*, in which an individual Supreme Court justice grants a stay or the whole Court offers a last-minute decision on whether its requirements against arbitrary infliction have been met, did not diminish. In a previous case in Florida involving Robert Sullivan, who had been on death row for ten years, Chief Justice Warren Burger charged Sullivan's lawyers with making "a sporting contest" of the criminal justice system.

It was evident that the Court was now intent on making speedier progress on executions. Besides Justice Burger in *Sullivan*, Justice Rehnquist, as noted previously, had also expressed impatience with the process. Justice Lewis F. Powell even declared in a speech that unless executions could proceed in a more orderly and acceptable fashion, without "irresponsible appeals," he would favor doing away with the death penalty altogether.

Some criticized the Court for being too intent on clearing out death row populations in U.S. prisons; they claimed that the Court itself was responsible for the confusion and that the standards set by *Furman* and earlier decisions lacked the incisive clarity needed to proceed. Defense lawyers primarily involved with capital cases have also complained about the rush to executions. They lamented that they did not have the time to devise proper strategies. The absence of qualified lawyers idealistic enough to handle the low-paying and thankless job of defending murderers—particularly in states with high rates of occupancy of death cells—led the American Bar Association to set up special programs.

To judge by the Court's divided *Furman* decision, and by its tentative decisions before and its restrictive ones afterward, deciding on the death penalty ranks among the more pernicious and tenacious of the Court's problems. The Court's main function is not to agonize over staying certain executions but to pass on the large issues in cases that the justices agree to consider and review and for which lower courts have failed to find satisfactory formulas. The highest court is bound to resolve such matters, even if only temporarily.

Ironically, the names of murder victims are forgotten, while those of their murderers live on in the epochal decisions of the higher courts.

Crucial Decisions before *Furman*

In 1968, four years before the sweeping *Furman* decision, the Court had ruled on a case involving William D. Witherspoon, whose crime consisted of ruthlessly killing a policeman. Witherspoon's lawyers had criticized the traditional practice of excluding jurors who were opposed to the death penalty. Since it was assumed that jurors who were willing to impose the death penalty would therefore tend to gravitate toward a guilty verdict, the Court ruled unconstitutional the practice of automatically excluding jurors opposed to the death penalty. The Court, however, made it plain that the inclusion of such individuals warranted close scrutiny. In seating jurors it was essential to determine whether their scruples were such that they would vote against capital punishment no matter what.

The judges steered a delicately balanced course. No, they said, opponents of the death penalty should not be automatically excluded from juries, as long as they were willing to *consider* all the penalties provided by state law and were not committed before the trial and presentation of evidence to voting against the penalty of death. In other words, anti–capital punishment jurors were to consider the law and the evidence and keep an open mind regardless of their general attitude toward the death penalty.[1] It was a tall—and perhaps un-realistic—order.

At least in theory an evenhanded Supreme Court struck down what was called death-qualifying a jury. A defendant thenceforth was entitled to a more representative jury, one that might include people with reservations about the death penalty.

The *Witherspoon* decision has been seen by some as a prelude to the far more important *Furman* decision. Rarely before, if ever, had the Court intervened in the procedures used in a case involving the death penalty. It did so again and again in the two decades that followed, although its decisions were never one-sidedly in favor of the accused or the prosecution.

The Court in *Witherspoon* also showed its awareness—though hardly the first time—of the difference between the death penalty and life imprisonment. At least one justice spoke of the finality of a capital judgment. Former chief justice John Harlan maintained that capital cases "stand on quite a different footing than other offenses." For him, "the law is especially sensitive to demands for that proce-dural fairness which inheres in a civil trial where the judge and trier of fact are not responsive to the command of the convening author-ity." He concluded by refusing to concede "that whatever process is 'due' an offender faced with a fine or a prison sentence necessarily satisfies the requirements of the Constitution in a capital case."[2]

Eliminating the death-qualifying practice led to a number of prisoners' death sentences being commuted or to their receiving new hearings that would resentence them.

In the post-*Furman* period, the proper composition of a jury, with all segments of the community represented, continued to be a source of appeals. In these cases, the poor representation of minority groups on juries had been seen as grounds for appeal, both in relation to the verdict and the sentence of death that was imposed. The Court was generally willing to consider these appeals, and it tended to side with the defense.

It began to appear that the Court would not be willing to consider the death penalty "cruel and unusual punishment" on any grounds. To be sure, a 1971 case, *McGautha v. California* was not based on the Eighth and Fourteenth amendments, which assure all U.S. citizens due process and fair and equal treatment, as *Furman* was. Still, there was a similarity to *Furman* in that McGautha claimed that neither the legislature nor the California courts provided adequate standards to guide a jury in choosing between death or life imprisonment for a defendant found guilty of first-degree murder. As a result, the imposition of the death penalty might sometimes be arbitrary. The Court ultimately ruled against McGautha, asserting that a comprehensive list of guidelines was impossible. Moreover, such a list might limit a jury in dealing with the many aspects of each case and, in fact, force it to impose the death penalty when without restrictive guidelines it might not do so. It was necessary for the states only to "follow procedures that are designed to assure reliability in sentencing determinations," according to Justice Powell, writing in another case. The Court affirmed the death sentence for McGautha (who had murdered in the course of an armed robbery), even though it made plain that it was not being asked to rule, and was not ruling, on the death penalty itself, but only on the "standards for guiding the sentencing authority's discretion."[3]

Thus, although the Court approved broad discretion in the *McGautha* decision, it rejected precisely that in the *Furman* case the following year.

Furman and Its Aftermath

On June 29, 1972, the Supreme Court officially announced its first ruling ever on the death penalty itself. The Court opined that

---

**"Moratorium" on Executions
Chronology**

1968: Executions cease in anticipation of ruling on constitutionality.

1972: June 29. Supreme Court rules on Georgia non-mandatory death verdict in *Furman*. Decision based on assumption that judges and juries were acting discriminatorily and capriciously in imposing the death penalty, a punishment deemed "cruel and unusual" under the Eighth Amendment and without "equal protection" and "due process" of the law under the Fourteenth Amendment.

1972–1976: State statutes in thirty-six jurisdictions reinstitute capital punishment as consistent with *Furman* ruling. Mandatory death sentences unauthorized almost everywhere.

1976: *Gregg v. Georgia*. Supreme Court upholds certain capital statutes imposing the death penalty for murder with the weighing of mitigating and aggravating factors, leaving the death penalty legally permissible in most jurisdictions.

1976: *Woodson v. North Carolina*. Supreme Court strikes down mandatory death sentence for murder.

1977: *Roberts v. Louisiana*. Supreme Court prohibits mandatory death ruling also for murder of a police officer. In this case and *Woodson* the Court argued that the Constitution called for "individualizing sentencing determinations" and "consideration of whatever mitigating circumstances may be relevant," formerly impossible under state statutes mandating the death penalty.

1977: Executions resume with the execution by firing squad of Gary Gilmore at his own request.

"imposition and carrying out of the death penalty . . . constitutes cruel and unusual punishment in violation of the Eighth and Fourteenth Amendments."[4]

There was wide jubilation in the ranks of the abolitionists. The jubilation soon died down, however, as lawyers and others critically examined the nine separate opinions handed down by the Court. They read, among others, Chief Justice Burger's dissenting view.

Two of the other opinions, he pointed out, opposed capital punishment only because of the way it was administered—"in a random and unpredictable manner." (Other opinions listed capriciousness, lack of standards, unfettered discretion, and so on.) If its administration was the source of the unconstitutionality of the death penalty, Justice Burger indicated how legislative bodies might seek to bring their laws into compliance with the Court's ruling by providing standards for juries.

Provided with this clear hint of how the death penalty might yet be regarded as constitutional, state legislatures—animated by a rising crime wave and a citizenry that saw the death penalty as necessary retribution—rushed to meet the popular demand. All that had to be done was to find formulas according to which arbitrariness, unbridled discretion, and discrimination could be inhibited, narrowed, or eliminated. Ways could be found to make the death penalty acceptable to all but two members of the Court—Justices Brennan and Marshall—who believed the death penalty to be inherently unconstitutional under the Eighth and Fourteenth amendments.

Over thirty state legislatures sought to bring their capital punishment statutes into accord with principles laid down by the Court's majority. Some of them offered guidelines that were unambiguous and consistent in some ways but highly questionable and ineffective in others. This group decided to make the death sentence mandatory for everyone found guilty of a certain clearly defined crime or crimes (despite the many problems associated with such a move). Another group of states complied with the Court requirement of holding a sentence hearing following a verdict of guilty. The hearing would be a continuation of the trial and yet in a sense separate from it. After someone was found guilty of murder in the first degree, a judge (in some states) or a jury (in others, depending on their statutes) could listen to any special aggravating or mitigating circumstances that affected the sentence.[5]

Soon the rewritten statutes that were in supposed compliance with the Court's ruling were themselves the subjects of litigation. Both types of statute were quickly challenged by lawyers intent on proving that even under the new procedures, their clients were still victims of cruel and unusual punishment. In some instances, in some states, death sentences were actually passed more readily now than they had been before *Furman*. With the exception of Gary

Gilmore in 1977 (whose death was called a suicide by some rather than an execution), however, no one had been executed since 1968, as the Court pondered compliance with its directives in the new state laws. There were then only three more executions between 1979 and 1981, making a grand total of only four executions in thirteen years.

The next rulings announced were surprisingly consistent. The statutes that had provided for a mandatory death sentence (as in *Woodson v. North Carolina*, 1976, and *Roberts v. Louisiana*, 1976) the Court threw out as unconstitutional—despite the statement in *Woodson* that, upon the adoption of the Bill of Rights, "the States uniformly followed the common law practice" of mandatory death sentences and that, in fact, this practice had not often been followed. According to Justice Marshall, this mandatory sentence in effect inhibits a judicial counterruling; the states had simply gone overboard and not allowed for any discretion at all. They were held to be in violation of the Eighth Amendment, which ostensibly prohibits cruel and unusual punishment.

On the other hand, the statutes of the second group of states, which had chosen the course of holding separate sentence hearings that carefully examined special circumstances that might impinge on the sentence, met the Court's test. Here the death penalty stood as it had before *Furman*, while far greater care would be taken in sentencing, with all possible facets of the case properly assessed. The statutes of Georgia, for example, would tend to lead to proper discretion, to limit arbitrary judgments, and to eschew the capriciousness that some of the justices in *Furman* had found unacceptable in cases involving life-and-death judgments. The Court found it necessary to remind the judicial world, and perhaps abolitionists in particular, that "the death penalty is not a punishment that may never be imposed, regardless of the circumstances of the defense, regardless of the procedure followed, in reaching a decision."[6]

The Supreme Court since *Furman* has made every effort, while retaining the death penalty, to make it fair, but some people maintain that it simply can never be made fair. There are many way stations on the criminal justice road, from the moment of arrest to the moment of execution, and there may well be points at which future litigation may occur over the discretion used, the thoughtful balance shown, the attempt at consistency, and the fairness in evidence.

Supreme Court Decisions Seen as Narrowing *Furman*

In the late 1970s Robert Harris and his brother (who had records that included manslaughter, sodomy, possession of weapons while in prison, and more) killed two teenage boys in California as they took the boys' car for a getaway after a bank robbery. They were soon caught and convicted of first-degree murder. In a separate sentence hearing, such as had been legitimated by the Supreme Court, the jury sentenced Robert Harris to death. The judge refused to go against the jury's judgment.

Harris's lawyers took the case up to the Supreme Court, claiming his sentence was out of proportion to those of others convicted of similar crimes. On occasion, various courts had previously accepted the proportionality argument and had changed a death sentence to life imprisonment—and the U.S. Ninth Circuit Court of Appeals agreed with Harris. But the U.S. Supreme Court, in *Pulley v. Harris* (1984), reversed the lower court decision, ruling by a seven-to-two majority (as always, with Marshall and Brennan dissenting) that proportionality reviews were not constitutionally required to prevent the discriminatory and arbitrary application of capital punishment. Writing the majority opinion, Justice White (who had been troubled by the question) declared that any capital sentencing scheme may "occasionally produce aberrational outcomes" but that in this case they were far removed from the major "systemic defects" that had been decried in *Furman*.

Not all observers agreed that the decisions of 1976–77 (for example, *Gregg v. Georgia*, *Profitt v. Florida*, etc.) were all that different from the conditions prevailing before *Furman*. Some maintained that the Court had gone full circle and had sufficiently modified and circumscribed the *Furman* decision to make it substantially less significant than it had appeared initially—or in the years immediately following.

While these abolitionists had solid reason for their disappointment, it should be said in fairness to the Court that, short of abolishing the death penalty—which for one reason or another all but Justices Marshall and Brennan opposed—it sought to steer a delicate course between maintaining the death penalty and making it substantially more difficult to impose. In ruling on different criteria required by the different states, the Court, by ruling now one way, now the other, seemed to be vacillating. On the one hand, it refused to outlaw the death penalty; on the other, it found the difficulty of making its imposition nonarbitrary, nondiscriminatory, and discretionary—yet just enough to keep it a viable punishment—nearly insurmountable. In seeking to overcome the quandary, and given the shortcomings of language, the Court's decisions at times seemed contradictory and retrogressive.

It is not our purpose here to summarize the nature or significance of the rulings handed down by the Court. We may simply say that it set aside some death penalty statutes and affirmed others. Yet there were decisions that in one way or another tended to confirm the Court's dimly recognizable twin goals, and to these we now turn.

Coker v. Georgia

Ehrlich Anthony Coker was an inmate who was serving three consecutive life terms for murder, rape, and kidnapping. He managed to escape from prison and had raped a sixteen-year-old girl before he was apprehended. The Supreme Court agreed to review the case. By a vote of seven to two, with then–chief justice Burger and Justice Rehnquist dissenting, it rejected the death penalty in this case on June 29, 1977, even though Coker was a notorious repeater and an obvious menace to society.

The Court declared in essence that, while rape undoubtedly deserves serious punishment, it does not involve the taking of human life. For a murder victim, life is over, but not for a rape victim, whose life may not be normal afterward but is "not beyond repair." The death penalty, being unique in its severity and irrevocability, therefore struck the Court as excessive for a rapist who does not take a human life. (The Court did not comment on what appeared to be reverse proportionality, since Coker had not received the death penalty for his earlier murder or for murder *and* rape.) Burger and Rehnquist, strict constructionists in their constitutional views, stated in their dissent that rape is a serious enough offense if state legislatures elect to regard it as deserving the death penalty.

The Court also declared in 1977 that kidnapping does not warrant the death penalty, leaving only murder, and possibly treason, as offenses serious enough to warrant capital punishment.

Lockett v. Ohio

Sandra Lockett had been involved in the murder of a pawnshop
owner in Ohio. She had not pulled the trigger and had not been on
the actual scene of the crime. But she had helped plan the robbery—
there had been no intent to murder—and she had driven the getaway
car. Youthful, misguided, and not too bright, she had also hidden
her companions.

Under Ohio law, the death penalty had to be imposed on Lockett
since three specific conditions for a milder sentence had not been
met. The judge had no choice; having been found guilty, she was
sentenced to death.

Her lawyers appealed, claiming that the three conditions provided for in the Ohio death-sentence statute were too narrow and
deprived the sentencing judge of a full opportunity to consider mitigating circumstances.[7] The Court agreed. Restricting a broad range
of mitigating circumstances, as the Ohio statute did, "creates the
risk," wrote Chief Justice Burger in 1978 in the majority opinion,
"that the death penalty will be imposed in spite of factors that may
call for a less severe penalty."[8] When the choice is between life and
death, Burger continued, this risk is unacceptable and is incompati-
ble with the requirements of the Eighth and Fourteenth amendments. The Court therefore found the Ohio statute unconstitutional.

Beck v. Alabama

In this case, decided in 1980, the range of choices open to the judge
under Alabama law was extremely narrow: he could either convict
the defendant, Gilbert Beck, of a capital crime, or acquit him.

Beck had participated with a companion in entering the home of
Roy Malone. He had not intended to kill Malone, nor had he known
or approved of the sudden impulse of his companion to kill Malone.
But he was nevertheless convicted of a capital offense under the Alabama statute for "robbery or attempts thereof when the victim is
intentionally killed [*sic*] by the defendant."[9] Beck appealed. The Supreme Court accepted his claim that a lesser charge should have been
available. The defendant was obviously guilty of a serious violent
offense, the Court held, but the case left some doubt in justifying
his conviction of a capital offense. The failure to offer the jury a third

alternative—namely, conviction on a lesser charge—enhanced the risk of an unwarranted capital-offense conviction. The Court again concluded that such a risk is intolerable when a human life is at stake.

Eddings v. Oklahoma

Young Monty Lee Eddings had proclaimed to his companion, as they were driving in a car, that he would "blow away" the police officer who was asking him to pull over to the side. Upon being stopped, Eddings killed the officer and, though a minor, was sentenced to death. At the sentence hearing following conviction, Eddings's lawyer presented a distressing picture of the boy's background: he had experienced beatings by a cruel father and had shown disturbed behavior in school and at home. Under Oklahoma law, the only mitigating circumstance that the judge could consider was the defendant's youth—he was only sixteen years old when he committed the crime—but this circumstance did not outweigh the aggravating circumstances. The Oklahoma Court of Criminal Appeals affirmed.

The Supreme Court vacated the death sentence, declaring that no mitigating factors could be excluded from consideration as a matter of law. All aspects needed to be considered, even if they were not necessarily accepted as sufficient.

The Court took pains not to question the state's decision to try him as an adult and stopped far short of suggesting that there is any constitutional proscription against imposing the death penalty on a person who is under age eighteen when he or she commits a murder.

While the Court did not rule on this issue in *Eddings v. Oklahoma*, the Court did rule on June 26, 1989, in separate 5 to 4 decisions, that states may impose the death penalty on mentally retarded and on youth who commit crimes as early as age sixteen.

The Court has been asked to consider these and other issues. It has agreed to look at some and not at others. Clearly, the question of mitigating circumstances has not been fully exhausted by its decisions to date.

Just as clearly, questions pertaining to the insanity defense as a mitigating circumstance will require further clarification. For example: What is the role of the psychiatrist? What is the state of his knowledge? How can one psychiatrist's "expert opinion" be meaningful when another psychiatrist with "equal expertise" comes to a different conclusion? Can the view of a person's behavior by a non-expert be admitted into evidence?

The Court has already ruled on facets of all these problems, while leaving itself room for further consideration in the future. The subject of mitigating circumstances, of defining and redefining discretion at different levels of the judicial process, the nature of a judge's instructions to the jury, the difference between a judge and a jury determining sentence, the method of execution, the participation of physicians in the administration of lethal injections—all of these, and many as yet unanticipated issues, will have to be resolved. But the fine distinctions, the subtle courses of action, the hairline-thin differentiations in decision making that challenge language itself to the utmost and expose its fallibility may still not yield the results for which the essentially fair-minded men and woman on the Supreme Court are striving.

Only two justices appear to have had a relatively easy time of coming to their decisions. Justices Thurgood Marshall and William J. Brennan, Jr., are both unalterably opposed to capital punishment as unfair, discriminatory, and unable to achieve the clarity and consistency required when a person's life is at stake. They have consistently voted against any decision that would further what for them is per se and intrinsically cruel and unusual punishment and therefore unconstitutional.

No one can question the sincerity and humanity of the Court, unless one looks upon executions as inherently inhuman. In all of its decisions, on whatever facet was under discussion, the Court has been aware of the finality and irrevocability of the death penalty. Again and again, it has written of the risks involved in not considering every factor that would allow death penalty decisions to be made on the soundest possible basis.

It remains to be seen whether the Court can find such a basis.

5

Deterrence: The Arguments and the Evidence

Fear is the mother of safety.

— Sir Francis Bacon

Fear is the parent of cruelty.

— J. A. Froude

S OME time ago, a Texas journalist who had seen nearly two hundred persons die in the electric chair over nearly three decades declared that the death penalty is not a deterrent—the prime merit claimed for it. "The only person it deters," he avers, "is the man being executed."

Yet deterrence remains the most important argument generally advanced by proponents of the death penalty in its favor. Other arguments—based on retribution, economic factors, and utilitarian factors—sound callous in the twentieth century (although for many they are still preeminent considerations). Deterrence, or preventing criminals and would-be criminals from committing murder, at least has a strong humanitarian component. Innocent lives will be saved, the reasoning goes, if criminals are aware of what lies in store for them if and when they are apprehended. Opponents of the death penalty flatly deny that there is any valid, acceptable evidence that capital punishment—and perhaps any other—genuinely deters people from committing crimes.

There is no lack of opinion—not even of formal research studies—addressing the question. But the evidence has hardly been conclusive. It is difficult even to imagine a controlled experiment that could prove that for every criminal executed, a given number of lives have been saved.

One's own response to the question "Does the death penalty deter?" depends on one's general attitude toward life and its problems. Those of us who tend to follow our hunches and who believe in the validity of common sense may well respond in the affirmative. After all, most of us would have bad dreams if it was even remotely suggested that we would be embroiled in a crime, found guilty, and executed.

But murderers are not like most people, except in that they are human. Murdering—killing—is deviant behavior, improbable behavior, unpredictable behavior. It is not likely, therefore, that before committing a crime, a murderer has nightmares about the prospect of a murder trial, a conviction, and death by whatever means. It may not even enter his consciousness. He may be indifferent to the consequences of his actions to himself. In other words, although the death penalty may "deter" average individuals from doing anything heinous, cruel, and murderous, it does not necessarily have a similar effect on actual killers or would-be killers. The Connecticut father who killed his son in a fit of rage over a television program was hardly thinking of what might happen to him—death or imprisonment—as a result of doing this incredible deed.

The criminal who accompanied Gilbert Beck into the home of Roy Malone, who helped tie him up, and who then suddenly, without warning, killed Malone, was a habitual offender, to be sure. But he was not a habitual killer. Yet suddenly, acting on a dark, inexplicable impulse, he killed. Was he thinking that he might be tried, convicted, and executed? Was he thinking at all?

What about the many killers who have no records of previously killing and who have no known desires or capacities for killing, but who, during a mugging or a holdup, notice an unexpected movement on the part of their victim and plunge a knife into the person, or shoot him or her out of fear? Do such killers even have the time to ponder the consequences? Is this willful murder or an impetuous, "defensive murder"?

What about repeat killers? They are often cited in other arguments in favor of retaining the death penalty. But are they ever deterred by the prospect of even the possibility of their own death?

Normal people would certainly consider the prospect of death while rationally contemplating a killing, if they had time. But normal people generally don't commit heinous crimes, except perhaps in cases of passion. The potential for doing evil may lie in all of us, but the death penalty is not what restrains us from acting on that potential. Normal people have a moral deterrent, as a result of proper socialization and of the development of conscience.

Those who make use of the deterrence argument in favor of retaining the death penalty often cite loose statistics to prove its effectiveness, statistics that appeal to common sense. For example, they argue that during the eight-year period, 1968 to 1976, when no executions took place in the United States, the number of murders rose at an alarming rate—in fact, it nearly doubled.[1] This is supposed to prove that there is a clear-cut relationship between the use of the death penalty and the incidence of murder.

But social scientists are substantially less certain that these statistics prove that such a relationship exists. Why single out one factor, the death penalty, to explain the increased murder rate? they ask. Could not a host of other factors have played a significant role? Why not consider, for instance, the terrifying increase in drug use that occurred during those years, and the fact that drug users must sometimes resort to crime to pay for their drugs? Why not consider the breakdown of values—the "thrill-killings" committed by the young and rich? Why not consider the ready availability of the tools of murder, the "Saturday Night specials," the sawed-off shotguns, the tools for stabbing and poisoning, and other means of killing? Why not consider the regulations and requirements needed to secure a gun license? Why not ask whether the individuals who applied for such a license were thoroughly checked for possible "priors," criminal records, and histories of mental or emotional illness?

Why not consider changes in social conditions that occurred during the period in question? Did the number of people living in poverty increase, creating a more devil-may-care attitude vis-à-vis crime? (Let us not forget the dictum of the great playwright, Bertolt Brecht: "First stuff your stomach—only then can you think morality.") Why not consider the increase in broken homes, the loss of desirable role models, the increasing resentment of the young at being emotionally deprived? Why not consider the possible decline in discipline in the home and at school? Why not consider the decline in religion and the often less-than-inspiring and unsavory conduct of many religious leaders? Why not consider the rise of indifferentism and cynicism among young people that we see reported nightly on television news programs and that upsets even mature adults? Last but not least, why not consider the increase in violence in television programs and movies? Does violence in story line after story line, program after program, beget violence? Can impressionable young-sters remain immune to depictions of shootings, stabbings, garrot-ings, fatal car chases, and other sorts of mayhem? In fact, have these graphic depictions of violence and of creative methods for killing one's enemies invited imitation? Has the increased incidence of TV deaths made crime into an everyday, "regular" occurrence rather than the abomination it was throughout history?

Indeed, one must ask, why single out the temporary absence of the death penalty as the sole—or even the primary—cause of the increased murder rate when there are so many other candidates for the honor? And finally, are not all these factors combined far more likely to have caused the wave of murders that has made our streets and even our homes unsafe?

Yet such suspicions, intuition, probabilities, and possibilities hardly provide reliable information. We must examine what social scientists, with reliable research tools at their command, have told us about the death penalty as a deterrent.

Studies of the death penalty that social scientists have under-taken have generally been of several varieties. One type of study makes comparative analyses of homicide rates for states that have different legal provisions for capital punishment. A second type of study analyzes murder rates just before and immediately after news stories that an execution or executions have occurred. A third type of study compares homicide rates before and after the abolition or reintroduction of the death penalty.

One of the best-known and most highly regarded studies on de-terrence was conducted by Thorsten Sellin, of the University of Pennsylvania. Sellin approached the question by examining homi-cide statistics in various clusters of adjacent states. The populations in the states shared ethnic, religious, economic factors in common. But in each cluster there were some states that had abolished capital punishment and others that had retained it.

Sellin's study emphatically concluded that the presence of the death penalty had no effect on the murder rates in the states examined.[2] In his matched group comparisons, capital punishment did not seem to influence the reported homicide rates in the least. But Ernest van den Haag has questioned Sellin's conclusions, pointing out that there is nothing in Sellin's tables that actually proves his case. Van den Haag also points to the "wild gyrations" that led to a 100 percent increase in Michigan's homicide rate within the space of a mere five years—and "without any changes in the threatened punishment." He insists that there is no explanation for these gyrations.[3]

Sellin and his fellow researchers such as Karl Schuessler and E. Sutherland have consistently maintained that abolitionist states have approximately the same or perhaps slightly lower homicide rates than neighboring states where the death penalty is intact.

Sellin has been the most emphatic. He found no relationship between large numbers of executions, small numbers of executions, continuous executions, no executions—and homicide rates. He has found further statistical support for his contention in the fact that between 1919 and 1934, the rate at which police were murdered in retentionist jurisdictions was 1.3 percent in 182 cities (Chicago excluded), whereas it was 1.2 percent per 100,000 population in 82 abolitionist cities.[4]

Sellin's and others' statistical investigations were considered in the *Furman* and *Gregg* cases. But some justices who were impressed by this type of evidence at the time of *Furman* rejected it four years later. By that time justices such as Lewis Powell were more apt to quote from the report of the British Royal Commission.

The most the Royal Commission could say about the question of deterrence was that the death penalty has "a stronger effect as a deterrent to normal human beings than any other form of punishment."[5] Responding to fears expressed by British police that their safety would be threatened if the death penalty were abolished, the Commission stated that it had no evidence that the abolition of capital punishment in other countries had in fact led to consequences feared by the British police.[6] On the contrary, "Austrian police claimed that the presence of the death penalty in the law offered such a threat to certain types of offenders that they would go to the extreme in attempting to avoid capture, and that, if the death penalty were removed, there would be less danger for the police."[7] (This argument cannot be used by abolitionists, however, for it presumes that criminals are aware of and consider the death penalty, an assumption not usually made.)

In examining all forms of evidence, the commission concluded that there is "no clear evidence [in Britain] in any of the figures we have examined that the abolition of capital punishment has led to an increase in the homicide rate or that its re-introduction has led to a fall."[8]

The major statistical investigations of deterrence have been undertaken by scholars friendly to the abolitionist cause. This is not to imply that in conducting their studies they were not animated principally by concern for truth (limited though that truth may be in the human sciences). Nor have they claimed that their studies are the last word on the subject of deterrence or that they have found the ultimate formula for investigating an elusive phenomenon. Still, theirs are the best and often the only studies that have seen the light of day, and they point clearly in one direction.

Even such enemies of the death penalty as Tufts's Hugo Adam Bedau recognizes that the studies supply only the best evidence to date and that their results hardly constitute perfect evidence. For example, during the research in many studies, not all factors lent themselves to adequate control or to perfect matching. As one element came under stricter control, it would sometimes turn others, previously controlled, into variables. Like many studies in the social sciences, the deterrence studies were subjected to questions about their data base, their application of statistical techniques, their measuring of important variables, and weaknesses in their analyses leading to their conclusions.

Bedau admits that imperfections in deterrence studies may have led to conclusions favorable to his cause. But he maintains that those who claim that capital punishment has deterrence value have the responsibility to prove their thesis. However, they have not done so: "None has ever published research tending to show, however inconclusively, that the death penalty is a deterrent and a superior deterrent to life imprisonment."[9] Retentionists' purely negative role as critics of admittedly less-than-ideal studies is apparently insufficient to prove their case; so is a partially true statement made by retentionist van den Haag. "Lack of proof does not amount to disproof," wrote this social philosopher and psychotherapist.[10] True, said some, but this is hardly a satisfactory approach.

Finally, in 1975, a study appeared that claimed to have found a relationship between executions and deterrence. Its author was an economist, Isaac Ehrlich, and his report, "The Deterrent Effect of Capital Punishment: A Question of Life and Death," was published, oddly enough, in the *American Economic Review.* The study might well have gone unnoticed in this unusual home. But it was brought to the attention of the legal and scholarly community—and by no less an authority than the then–solicitor general of the United States, Robert H. Bork. In an amicus curiae brief Bork filed with the Supreme Court in *Fowler v. North Carolina,* he mentioned the Ehrlich study and claimed that it supplies vital empirical support "for the *a priori* logical belief that the use of the death penalty decreases the number of murders."[11]

The Ehrlich study concluded that during the period 1933–67 in the United States, "On the average the tradeoff between the execution of an offender and the lives of potential victims it might have saved was of the order of magnitude of 1 for 8." (This is often interpreted to mean that each execution deterred as many as eight murders).[12] Retentionists were delighted at this evidence to support their side, but abolitionists rejected the study as "outrageous, pure garbage, deliberate deception."

The techniques used by Ehrlich and Sellin were fundamentally different from each other. Sellin relied on data from selected pairs of states; Ehrlich worked out a time-series analysis from data gathered throughout the United States. Both of these methods are imperfect for dealing not only with a multitude of social, geographic, cultural, and demographic variables but also with temporal variables that change from generation to generation, year to year, week to week, and even day to day. Ehrlich himself never claimed that his research proved the deterrent effect of capital punishment, but he insisted that his work take no back seat to any other study published up to that point.

Walter Berns, an avowed retentionist and a balanced admirer of Ehrlich's investigations, assessed Ehrlich's work, and he reopened the question of deterrence after Sellin's report. "No one can now say that it is *known* that the death penalty is not a more effective deterrent," he averred.[13]

At the same time, no one can claim that Ehrlich's study even comes close to conclusively resolving the question, certainly no closer than Sellin's more widely known and understood work. Evidently, social science cannot satisfactorily devise studies that can answer the deterrence question once and for all. This absence leaves the advantage with the retentionists, for it forces the issue to remain in the realm of hunch and common sense.

Sometimes it is difficult to understand why there are two definite sides to a matter of such importance, and why the "normal" people who carry out such studies get so worked up about an issue in which they have no vital, personal stake. This is not to diminish their efforts on behalf of protecting society, nor to understate the necessity of building morality. It is simply to be amazed that honest, bipartisan studies cannot be undertaken with a view to finding an answer, however tenuous or unpleasant it may turn out to be for either side, and then to work together for a solution to the many obviously underlying causes of serious crime.

There is evidence both for and against deterrence that somehow lingers between the intuitive and the scientific varieties; that is, evidence that has some professional if not expert opinion behind it. One example is that of the longtime warden of Sing Sing prison in New York State, Lewis E. Lawes. Lawes was present at over 150 executions; in fact, it was his dubious privilege to lead those condemned persons to the electric chair. According to Lawes, none of the doomed persons said that they had given any thought whatever to the death penalty when they committed their act of murder. Of course, this informal observation does not constitute scientific evidence; we do not know whether they were actually questioned and if so, how.

There are other sources of informal evidence that challenge the deterrence claim. In his *Reflections on Hanging*, Arthur Koestler (who was himself under sentence of death in Spain during that country's civil war) quotes an eighteenth-century murderer, George Manley, shortly before the latter's execution: "My friends, you assemble to see—what? A man leap into the abyss of death. You see what I am—a little fellow. My Redeemer knows that murder was far from my heart and what I did was through rage and passion being provoked by the deceased. You say I killed a man. Marlborough killed his thousands and Alexander his millions. I'm a little murderer and must be hanged. How many men were lost in Italy and upon the Rhine during the last war for killing a king in Poland? Both sides could not be right—but I killed a solitary man."[14]

Former warden of Sing Sing prison, Lewis Lawes, an abolitionist, cites the story of the operator of the guillotine in French Guiana, a certain Hospel, who was surely more aware than most of the price of murder. Yet he proceeded to murder on his own and was himself executed. According to FBI statistics, most murders are crimes of passion. People who kill in passion are neither aware of nor concerned about either punishment or even getting caught.

One widely known student of the death penalty, Dr. Raymond T. Bye, tells of a Pennsylvania man who witnessed an execution and on the same day committed a murder. Far from deterring murders, Bye theorizes, executions exert an unpredictable and suggestive influence on "weak-minded" individuals.

Similarly, Ezzrat Abdel Fattah, a professor of criminology at the University of Montreal, concludes in his study that there is no deterrence factor to the death penalty. Instead, he claims, the most important factor in deterrence is the certainty of punishment—the very thing that is missing from the American system of justice.

In a volume entitled *Reviving the Death Penalty*, Gary McCuen and R. A. Baumgart claim that countries that have abolished capital punishment actually have lower rates of murder and attempted murder. A New York study of murders between 1907 and 1960 shows that on average two additional homicides were committed in the month following an execution.[15]

Howard Zehr's 1984 "Death as a Penalty," published by the Mennonite Central Committee, states that even if the death penalty does deter, the deterrent effect is so small that "even the most sophisticated attempts have been unable to measure it." Capital punishment, he claims, is no more effective than imprisonment in deterring people from committing violent crimes. In fact, rather than preventing violence, capital punishment may have a "brutalizing effect" that tends to raise the general level of violence. Thus, its effect may be to raise—not to lower—murder rates.[16]

A Marlboro, Massachusetts, clergyman, the Reverend Philip A. Smith, testified before a state judiciary committee, "Those who favor keeping the death penalty are faced with an impossible dilemma. If they somehow succeed in using it more, the more dislike of it will spread; juries will become more difficult, convictions will drop, and increased pressure for its abolition will continue. If, on the other hand, those who favor the death penalty agree to using it sparingly, then they gravely weaken their argument, for the less it is used, the less its deterrent effect will become."[17] Smith admits—claims—that the death penalty has a deterrent effect. How can anyone "agree" to use the death penalty sparingly?

Informal proof plays an important role in the arguments of those who claim the death penalty has a deterrent effect. There has hardly been an absence of thinkers who demand retention of capital punishment, but the argument heard most often is that the lack of reliable proof for deterrence doesn't mean it doesn't exist. Thus, Norman Darwick, director of the International Association of Chiefs of Police, declared before the House Judiciary Committee on April 20, 1981, that statistical arguments are of limited value. "It has yet to be shown . . . that the death penalty is not more effective than other punishments. Failure to prove an effect does not mean that there is no effect." Darwick suggested that the more systematically murderers are eliminated by execution, the greater the deterrence effect will be and the more innocent lives will be saved.

In his testimony before the Senate Judiciary Committee on April 27, 1981, D. Lowell Jensen, of the criminal division of the U.S. Department of Justice, reverted to the commonsense "proof" for deterrence. Conceding that sociological studies have concluded otherwise, he said, "Common sense tells us that the death penalty does operate as an effective deterrent for some crimes involving premeditation and calculation, and that it thus will save the lives of persons who would otherwise become the permanent and irretrievable victims of criminal misconduct." He declared further that some offenses are so harmful and reprehensible that no other penalty—not even life imprisonment without the possibility of parole—would be adequate.

Retentionists sometimes quote Sir James Stephen of the British Royal Commission: "The fact that men are hanged is one reason why murder is considered to be so dreadful a crime." Just as abolitionists claim that all life is cheapened when the state takes a life, so retentionists maintain that life is cheapened if we don't impose a penalty on the taking of a life that is higher than those we impose on other crimes of violence and on crimes of property.

There is, however, one sure and powerful argument in favor of deterrence: capital punishment does deter those who are executed. Before one congressional committee, a police chief, Ed Davis, said, "You don't shoot a rabid dog to deter other rabid dogs; you shoot him so he won't bite somebody." Incapacitation is really not part of the deterrence argument. The deterrence argument basically concerns whether the execution of a rabid killer will prevent other potentially rabid killers from killing.

Ernest van den Haag, indisputably one of the most effective spokesmen for capital punishment, is concerned more with preserving the lives of innocent citizens. He drives home the point that since we do not know if anything deters murder, we ought to choose execution to protect the innocent.[18] His further, utilitarian point has horrified even some retentionists—namely, that the use of an extreme deterrent can be justified if it reduces the total number of innocent lives lost.

Advocates of the death penalty speak of "numerous cases" that are on record in which convicted murderers escaped the death penalty and then proceeded to commit new ones. (Also a genuine dilemma is the killing of one prison inmate by another. Whether there is any alternative punishment to the death penalty for such cases is questionable. Perhaps the prospect of solitary confinement would prove to be a deterrent.)

In the Supreme Court's decision on the case *Gregg v. Georgia*, all the justices (except Marshall and Brennan) agreed that the scientific evidence regarding deterrence was inconclusive. (They then reverted to the hunch theory of probability.) Only a few lines after saying this, however, the Court pronounced the death penalty an undoubtedly significant deterrent, except in crimes of passion. Individually, Justices White and Rehnquist have also spoken of the "useful penological function" of the death penalty, provided it is not imposed too seldom or too arbitrarily.

The arguments have not essentially changed—nor have their bases—in nearly two hundred years. In 1810, a chief justice in Britain is reported as arguing against a bill to abolish the death penalty for shoplifting. According to the justice, "Were the terror of death to be removed, it is my learned opinion that shops would be liable to unavoidable losses from depredations, and in many cases bankruptcy and ruin must become the lot of honest and laborious tradesmen."[19]

The evidence available to that justice was not much worse than the evidence available to us today (although we no longer prophesy such chaos if the death penalty were to disappear). We are almost certainly doomed to never knowing the facts about what the "deterrent effect" has been, is, and will be. No properly controlled experiment seems possible now or in the future; conditions do not remain static enough in time and place in any study in the social sciences. Not even the question of where in the deterrence argument the burden of proof lies has been resolved.

With the scientific evidence inconclusive, we may well be reduced to using hunches, as the Supreme Court itself has been in recent years. The normal person's hunch is based on identifying his or her own reaction to the prospect of execution as the same as the reactions of potential murderers. But reliance on nothing firmer than probabilities and possibilities and hunches is terrifying, considering the irrevocability of death.

The deterrence question was recently raised once again in regard to a proposal to impose the death penalty on drug dealers. The idea was very popular in Congress in 1988, especially after it was discovered that the public wanted a war on drugs in earnest and was generally supportive of the death penalty. On September 22, President Reagan said in Texas, "We believe that when a drug dealer kills a police officer in the line of duty, he should have to give up his life as punishment."

But drug kingpins normally operate in a world of violent death, and this world has apparently not deterred them so far. Indeed, competition and rivalry among dealers, frustration and anger on the part of addicts, and raids by drug enforcement officials have kept them solidly in business. Whether the prospect of execution by society would frighten them more than the old dangers do—especially considering their lucrative trade—is debatable.

Some retentionists (with a measure of seriousness) and some abolitionists (partly in jest) have suggested that returning to public executions would be a sure way to deter crime. There has even been a suggestion—half serious, half not—that for the death penalty to be a truly effective deterrent, some executions should be televised. After all, other horrors have been shown on television—gruesome accidents, people dying in war, the homeless perishing in gutters, drug addicts wasting away in cities; why not a public execution, or even a televised one? Perhaps it would really deter; perhaps it would not. It might be the one way to put the question to a real test.

Other observers insist that executions should not be televised but could nevertheless be made public in a somewhat restricted sense. Presently, only a handful of persons witness executions; it strikes us as not unreasonable to add to that number at least several state representatives. After all, they are duly elected by the people and presumably carry the wishes of the people into law.

The justification of the death penalty may not reside in its deterrence value—if, indeed, it has any. It may finally be nothing less and nothing more than a philosophical matter.

6

Is the Death Penalty Cruel?

It is the crime which causes shame, not the scaffold.
— Thomas Corneille

All the perfumes of Arabia will not sweeten this hand.
— Shakespeare

W HEN convicted murderer James Autry was about to be executed in May 1984, he asked that the event be televised. Im-
plicitly blaming the public for his demise, he announced, "Now let
them find out what they have done." Autry's request renewed interest in the idea of public executions.

Proponents of capital punishment thought that public executions
might finally prove the deterrent capacity of capital punishment.
Opponents were convinced that the viewing public would be so re-
pelled by witnessing an execution such as Autry's that many would
become abolitionists.

There have been no public executions in the United States since
the last hanging in Texas in 1937. For the previous one, which took
place in Kentucky in 1936, over twenty thousand people are reported
to have gathered to see it. Some climbed onto poles, and others stood
on rooftops. Apparently, the theatrical appeal that executions held
in England for centuries did not die out as civilization advanced.

Autry's request was not filled by the authorities nor by the net-
works, normally eager for sensational events. One TV cameraman
made a legal effort to film Autry's death, but the request was turned
down.

Perhaps some had seen the fictionalized execution of Caryl

Chessman on television. Realistically portrayed by Alan Alda, the 1977 spectacle, called "Kill Me If You Can," terrified many and made one author of the present volume into a foe of capital punishment. Witnessing smoke issuing from a human head is different in nature from thinking about it in the safety of one's living room. It raises the question of the *cruelty* of capital punishment.

One may well ask whether the legal termination of a life by society itself can be construed cruel. "Cruel" and "unusual" are little more than abstract, relative terms in spite of the continued use of these adjectives in newspaper headlines.

In 1958, the Warren Court held that the Eighth Amendment's admonishment regarding "cruel and unusual" punishment signifies "evolving standards of decency that mark the progress of a maturing society." Just eighteen years later, practically on the eve of the nation's two-hundredth anniversary, the Supreme Court expressed the opinion that neither the Eighth nor the Fourteenth Amendment prohibits the exercise of capital punishment under all circumstances. However, a scant four years earlier in the *Furman* decision, the Court had proclaimed that the "arbitrariness and capriciousness" with which some death sentences were being imposed clearly constituted a form of cruel and unusual punishment. For some, it was an appreciably large semantic leap to connect the words *cruel* and *unusual* with a coordinating conjunction, for *cruel* and *unusual* are by no means equivalent, nor even necessarily degrees of one another. But it was considerably more of a leap to single out the death penalty for scrutiny. Others thought the ruling came at a time when the country was showing very few signs of maturity, particularly an obvious increase in lawlessness everywhere.

It may be remembered that only two justices believed capital punishment to be intrinsically cruel. The others agreed that only when unfairly and irresponsibly applied was it cruel and unusual. The majority of justices regarded neither the death penalty nor death itself as cruel and unusual, only the existing administration of that penalty. Hence, the *Furman* ruling was a constitutional decision and not a moral judgment on society's right to claim the lives of murderers.

Cruel is most often defined in dictionaries as "deliberately causing pain or distress to others, or enjoying the effects." *Unusual* means "not common or ordinary, uncommon in amount or degree; exceptional; rare." In the Eighth Amendment, *cruel and unusual* refers to the use of torture. Throughout history, the death penalty may well have been cruel; but until the sixth decade of this century it was certainly not unusual, although actual executions had become increasingly uncommon. We shall therefore consider only the question of cruelty here.

An execution involves an executioner; someone who was once a killer and who is now the victim of a killing; and the society in whose name the execution is taking place. Let us examine each of the components of the occasion.

The Executioner

In some times and in some places, such as France, the office of executioner was virtually hereditary. If the victim was of the French upper classes, the executioner wielded a swift, incisive sword that severed the head neatly from the body. If the victim was of the masses, an ax would be used to achieve a similar result, though the failure to kill immediately was more likely but less stressful to the public. On occasion, the aim of a senior French executioner would fall short of the mark, and in his frustration he would call upon his son to finish a job that, by then, had become messy. Executions in both France and England were frequent, and the métier of executioner was considered, if not honorable, certainly more respectable than it is today.

Not infrequently, however—in the French provinces and throughout England, where hanging was the preferred mode—the executioner was anonymous. As he performed his appointed task, he wore a hood to make identification difficult. Although the hangman's task was deemed necessary as retributive, deterrent, and just, he himself was often forced to live outside the community he served. Communities wanted no part of one who killed, for whatever reason, with whatever justice. Apparently not all executioners were wholly relaxed about their job. In numerous cases, executioners were reported as having to give themselves courage for their grisly deed by imbibing too much and then botching the job, having to try over and over again to put the victim to death.

In some non-Western societies, such as China, executioners seem to be even crasser than in the West. Before the death sentence is carried out, the executioner makes a deal with the condemned. If the latter is rich, the executioner will dispatch him or her with precision for a fee paid by relatives. If the person is poor, the executioner assures a quick death in exchange for the victim's clothes.

In our cultured society, the hangman as such has disappeared. A firing squad—in effect, multiple executioners—acceded to Gary Gilmore's wish for death by that method. When the electric chair or the gas chamber is used, the human connection is somewhat less direct, for pulling a switch or releasing a pellet avoids executioner-to-victim contact. The process is as simple as pulling a light switch or the lever of a fuse box, or lighting an electric or gas stove. The modern executioner does not touch the body of his victim and may become aware of him or her only when he sees the small assembly of invited observers. It is the attending physician who determines when the victim is dead. It is the physician who senses the magnitude of the deed, even though he did not perform the small mechanical action that led to the death. He observes the action in detail, verifies the outcome, and answers questions at the end.

In the newest style of execution—lethal injection—the physician participates in the act. Such participation could guarantee a swifter and more merciful end for a misspent life than that of a layman following directions. But recently, the medical associations have been calling medical participation in this kind of killing inappropriate because of the conflict with the Hippocratic oath. Indeed, physicians are already struggling with many moral dilemmas that have been produced by technology and that are related to the end of life; many regard involvement in executions as an impossible and unwanted burden and contrary to their essential task. Other physicians, however, reflect the attitude of the public at large. One of the authors of the present book asked one female and three male physicians of his acquaintance how they felt about the death penalty. All said that they could not throw the switch or administer the injection. But the men added that, speaking as ordinary citizens, they approved of and supported capital punishment. The woman disapproved of it altogether.

Throughout history executioners have sought to detach themselves from the act of killing and have not wanted to be known as society's hired killers, as agents in inflicting pain in less-than-perfect executions. Even if executioners do not see themselves as killers—

though at times they must, in spite of societal permission—society nevertheless regards them as persons capable of killing. Many people regard executioners with a secret awe, fear, and contempt—mixed with a bit of admiration. But they wonder, who would choose to earn his livelihood by accepting money for the act of killing? Executioners are also therefore suspected of being psychologically abnormal or deviants, or of having imperfectly developed consciences. They are seen, perhaps unfairly, as epitomizing cruelty—as people for whom cruelty is the highest pleasure and love. George Eliot's observation on cruelty seems to apply to them: "Cruelty, like every other vice, requires no motive outside of itself; it only requires opportunity."

The warden of a prison that has a "death row" often must act as an adjunct to the executioner, though it is not he who pulls the switch or releases the pellets or gives the injections. Unlike law enforcement officials, wardens in death-house prisons have generally tended not to support capital punishment. The reason may well lie in the fact that whereas policemen, prosecutors, and even judges are primarily concerned with the crime the person has committed, the warden meets the perpetrator sometime after he or she has been convicted. The former see the criminal only in relation to the crime; they see a horrendous deed and the animal in human form that did it. But the warden is more likely to recognize a residue of humanity, even if it is at the lowest levels; for him, such criminals are enemies of their own life and could not control and direct the evil that lies in us all.

The warden condones the crime no more than the policeman or the prosecutor, but in the prison situation the warden is at times reminded of tenuous links to humanity the murderer may still possess. The warden may experience ambivalence about guiding the death-bound individual through his or her final days, about providing him with his last meal, about keeping him posted concerning last-minute appeals, about having to tell him that they have been denied, about worrying that a reprieve will arrive a minute too late, about being kept in the dark about what is going on in the minds of judges and governors. He must be concerned that the execution proceeds without a hitch and that the equipment of death does not malfunction. He may not relish the task of accompanying the victim to the death site. He may wonder whether the person he is leading to execution is not being killed with as much—if not more—premeditation than the killer himself used.

The Killer-Victim

Historically, men—and sometimes women and children—were executed for reasons we now regard as questionable, but today's rare victim of execution is for the most part a brutal murderer whose record has been considered; the aggravating or mitigating circumstances of his crime have been assessed to the extent that human beings can do so with wisdom, impartiality, and perhaps compassion. The death penalty itself is imposed today only after a careful review of the facts both before the verdict and again, for purposes of sentencing, after the verdict. A person is condemned to death only after all these precautions have been taken to ensure a fair sentence under the law. Why one killer-victim is chosen to be executed among the hundred on death row who are equally guilty, criminal, and vicious is another question.

The Victim

In eight of the states that have death penalty statutes, a convicted killer may choose among various methods of execution, ranging from the firing squad to intravenous injection. The development of new modes of execution suggests that society has become increasingly aware of the need to kill mercifully, with as little pain to the killer-victim as possible. At present, lethal injection is regarded by some as the most nearly pain-free method. Of course, no prisoner has returned from the grave to confirm this, and each new method has its own ways to be bungled.

The average citizen in whose name the laws are passed may not be satisfied simply when "something has been done." Unlike the warden, the average citizen is not likely to attribute any vestiges of humanity to a criminal. He does not see a human being in his mind's eye; he sees only the letters in the word *murderer*. Or he sees a ruthless killer, like Willie Horton, whose crime on furlough in Massachusetts helped ruin the candidacy of a presidential contender.

For this mythical average citizen, the killer had it coming; he is getting his just deserts. This citizen may be the most devoted of parents and spouses, but when it comes to the criminal killer, he or she dismisses with impatience any notion of cruelty. It becomes a question of who engaged in cruelty first—and the answer is certainly the killer, who should therefore not become a burden or remain a threat to the community. The killer has forfeited any rights to human consideration. If legislators and elected officials nonetheless concern themselves with reducing cruelty, Mr. or Ms. Average Citizen goes along with it—with minimal interest and with a measure of impatience.

The question of the killer-victim's residual humanity—a poor humanity, but humanity nonetheless—rarely interests our average citizen and interests the legislator concerned about votes even less. Regard for residual humanity remains the concern of the intellectual, the do-gooder, the bleeding heart, the one who worries about the killer more than the individual who was killed. Our mythical average citizen dismisses concerns for cruelty, for pain willfully inflicted on another, largely because the killer has sacrificed any natural claim to normal human consideration.

Nor is this average citizen likely to be concerned—as former attorney general Ramsey Clark is—about the dignity of humankind in general or about the idea that humankind is somehow diminished by each execution. In his legitimate anger at crime in general and at one crime in particular, it is doubtful that the partisan of the death penalty worries much about the fabric of society.

George Bernard Shaw once wrote that "murder and capital punishment are not opposites that cancel one another, but similars that breed their kind."[1] It is not likely that this idea would have much influence on men and women equally sure that the laws of society are just and must be obeyed, that criminals are evildoers and murderers the worst criminals, and that it is the right and duty of society to punish criminals in accordance with their crime. Nor would they be greatly concerned about the dismay felt by inmates in prisons upon hearing that within their walls somebody has been electrocuted, gassed, or poisoned. Perhaps, the average citizen will say, the execution will serve as a deterrent to those in prison who are as close to the abyss as they may get. On the other hand, if they are serving out sentences of no more than a few months or a year, the stress of being in proximity to a judicial killing, of overidentifying with the person killed in the same house, may constitute cruel and perhaps even unusual punishment.

Maybe there is no way to look upon persons under sentence of death as much more than mere objects. In order that a legal error not be made, they are suspended between living and dying, sometimes for years. The intolerably long wait—necessary both for their own protection and for the integrity of the state—adds further cruelty to the death penalty, however unintended. Even if the condemned person is among the many who will not be executed, he or she will have suffered horrible anguish and experienced cruelty as defined.

There are conflicting, seriously adversarial views on whether the death penalty cheapens human life. Death penalty advocates have been emphatic: since people need and crave justice; since, moreover, people have created systems based on justice—it follows that someone who has murdered must be punished in relation to the seriousness of that crime. Since murder is a final, irremediable, irrevocable act, the punishment accorded the murderer can and must be also final, irremediable, and irrevocable. Failure to make it so would cheapen human life.

Death penalty opponents follow a different argument. The sacredness of life is violated if society deprives anyone of life, even one who previously deprived another of life. The initial act was a brutal, often heinous murder, and the penalty for it must be permanent incapacitation of the murderer. But killing the killer would be to inflict the same cruelty and brutality on the killer. Killing is brutal, cruel, execrable, whether it is done criminally by the murderer or legally by the state. In either case, life is cheapened in the post-Auschwitz, post-Hiroshima age that has witnessed enough cheapening of life.

The teachings of religion on the sanctity of life cut both ways. On the one hand, religion tells us, he who kills an innocent person is responsible for the blood of all the victim's potential descendants to the end of time. On the other hand, the Talmud accepts capital punishment but adds this admonition pertaining to cruelty: "Choose an easy death for him who must be executed."[2] While one rabbi termed a court murderous if it effected one execution in seven years, another put the number at seventy. One of the most famous rabbis of all time stated that if he had been a member of the Sanhedrin, no one would ever have been put to death.

Finally, in regard to the victim, we should not forget the statement of the late Supreme Court justice Benjamin Cardozo, who wrote in *Law and Literature,* "The death penalty will seem to the next generation as it seems to many even now, an anachronism too discordant to be suffered, mocking with grim reproaches all our clamorous professions of the sanctity of life."[3]

Society

Though the majority of Americans approve of the death penalty without necessarily knowing much about it, large segments of society are uneasy about its imposition. All want murderers to be out of the way, incapacitated, and at the same time punished for his or her crime in a "proportionate" manner. But most people, when called upon to sit on a jury and produce a verdict on a criminal whose atrocious deed they have heard discussed for days or weeks, become hesitant and at times squeamish. Nor would many responsible, rational, and strong-minded people wish to be present at an execution. In their innermost selves they want no part of the death scene, not even in the privacy of their minds. Although they feel revulsion at murder and crime and want to feel protected and safe, they want others—anonymous others—to deal with the dirty business of snuffing out the life of the criminal. Instinctively, many would agree that regardless of what method is employed, execution remains a dirty, cruel, painful, abominable business.

Ramsey Clark, a vehement foe of capital punishment, has written that "capital punishment harms everything it touches."[4] He has commented on the excruciatingly long waits on death row that, in his judgment, add immeasurably to the cruelty of capital punishment. Defense lawyers in capital cases, fully aware of the gravity of executing a human being, know that their clients' lives, however devalued by crime, rest heavily on their shoulders. They feel compelled to employ every technicality, every escape hatch. In some cases they keep trying even after the client himself has lost the desire to go on. The use of radical, unusual measures distorts the law, makes a mockery of the fact-finding process, and sensationalizes everything. Executions thus become a terrible burden upon society, even apart from the financial cost—which in a discussion of the sanctity of human life has no place at all.

Thus, we have the paradox of society demanding the death penalty to exact revenge and eliminate a criminal but at the same time people hesitating to take responsibility in individual cases as jurors or other functions. Implicit is the awareness that killers should pay the ultimate penalty, but that that penalty is evil and must be avoided.

Over the centuries society has reduced the number of capital offenses. In the United States, it has resolutely retained capital punishment on the books, but has been reluctant to carry the punishment through to its conclusion. Through the voting booth and in public opinion polls, it expresses insecurity and fears of damage by crime. Many of its more rational members endorse the efforts of legislators to find the least cruel and least barbaric method of execution, but they do not even want to hear details of the debate. The contrast between belief and behavior in large segments of society reveals that, even as the demand for capital punishment persists, the suspicion has dawned that executions by whatever method are barbaric and cruel. On the subject of moral choice, no decision is as yet possible between "an eye for an eye" on the one hand and "thou shalt not kill" on the other.

Proponents and opponents of the death penalty agree that willful murderers deserve the ultimate penalty; the preciousness of life dictates this. But they go distinctly separate ways in deciding what the ultimate penalty ought to be. Retentionists are willing to bear the moral weight of taking a life; abolitionists are not. Both take their positions in the name of the sanctity and preciousness of life.

The same pattern of agreement and disagreement permeates discussions of the methods of execution. Retentionists regret that taking a life is a necessity and wish to use the method that is most in accord with humaneness, as we best understand that term now. For abolitionists, who are also concerned with humaneness, no method of killing is humane.

The term *barbaric* has been applied most often to the act of snuffing out a human life. *Barbaric* means "without civilizing influence, primitive, savage." The death penalty, as we saw in chapter 2, originated in a primitive, often savage, state of civilization, when virtually every flaw and fault was punishable by death and when modes of killing were morbidly creative. As civilization advanced, the number of punishable offenses decreased markedly. Where the death penalty persists in advanced societies, it has been retained mostly for one to three crimes: murder, rape, and treason. The number of executions has also decreased in the West.

Methods of execution have also become more humane. In the United States, where thirty-nine states retain the death penalty, the methods vary from jurisdiction to jurisdiction. All seek to choose the method least offensive to the survivors and the one most humane for the killer-victim. In some instances, as we have seen, the latter are given a choice of method.

Perhaps at this point, in the manner of nineteenth-century novelists, we should stop and ask: dear reader, suppose you had committed a crime and were sentenced to death. Which of the following ways of doing away with yourself would you prefer? We have to kill you, but you may decide on the method of dying. Which of the following methods would you choose?

Hanging. This is a classic form of execution. It is hoped that the rope around your neck will break your neck. However, you may not be so fortunate. If the drop is too short, you will be slowly and painfully strangled. If the drop is too long, then the head may be severed from the body in a most brutal fashion.

Electric Chair. The American colonies never took to the guillotine the way the French did. The United States proceeded directly from hanging to the electric chair. In fact, at this writing, electrocution remains the commonest way of removing criminals from the scene. A brief description: you are led by the warden into the chamber that houses the chair. You are strapped into it; electrodes are attached to your head and legs. The current is set in motion; your body will strain. Smoke will issue from your head and perhaps from other parts of your body. Your flesh will burn, but you will probably no longer be aware of it.

To some of you this method may not be appealing; in fact, it may seem downright inhuman. Yet you are not being burned at the stake, as in medieval times; you are not being burned on a pyre.

Rather, currents of electricity burn your body to death from the inside out.

Gas Chamber. Another way of terminating you is possible; this is the more modern gas chamber. Here again, you will be neatly strapped into a chair; a container of sulfuric acid will be placed underneath you. After the "assistants" have made certain that the chamber is properly sealed, cyanide is dropped into the acid to produce the lethal gas. Soon the gas fills the chamber. Your eyes will pop, and you will turn purple. Perhaps you will drool. Again, it is difficult to foresee how long it will take you to lose consciousness. It may be a bit inconvenient for you as you desperately try to get air. Alas, you will not get it.

But rest assured, dear reader, that if you choose this method, your death will be similar to the deaths of millions of Jews, Poles, Ukrainians, and others in the gas chambers of Eastern Europe in World War II. They had done nothing to merit this destruction, of course, whereas you have committed an atrocious, unforgivable crime.

Lethal Injection. Dear reader, we would like to make clear that lethal injection has made the executioner's lot easier. Three persons are involved in opening the valves, and none knows which one is releasing the fatal dose. This latest method of execution may indeed have its advantages, but in December 1983 the press reported that Charlie Brooks had been executed by intravenous injections in Texas and that apparently he had experienced some pain. The press stated that a vein had been cannulated by a physician. Outside the chamber a mixture of chemicals was injected. One of these was to paralyze the muscles and another to stop the heart.

Shortly thereafter, a dentist in Metuchen, New Jersey, who was also a member of the New Jersey legislature, introduced a bill there approving lethal injection. The bill was passed and signed by Republican governor Thomas Kean. The dentist-assemblyman wanted a relatively painless method because it would be "less subject to criticism." Thus, it was mainly for the purpose of preserving capital punishment that Thomas H. Paterniti, D.D.S., was interested in proposing a more humane method. He wanted to demonstrate, moreover, that civilized people show murderers more compassion than the murderers displayed toward their victims.

According to the dentist-legislator, the killer-victim would be tranquilized or anesthetized by a narcotic or barbiturate just before the injection of the lethal dose. Dr. Paterniti gave further evidence of his compassion when he stipulated that the toxic shot be administered in such a fashion that the "executioner-technician" would not know whether he had delivered the fatal dose. Nor would the public know which of the technicians did the actual killing. In addition, the bill specified who would be permitted to be present at the execution.

In New Jersey, Dr. Paterniti said, there would be less pain for the victims of execution than there had been for Charlie Brooks in Texas.

Dear reader, would you not, if you had committed a dastardly crime, wish to suffer in New Jersey?

Firing Squad. Finally, you might wish to opt for the firing squad. Even if one or two of the shots miss your heart, others will strike home. It will be quick, merciful, and painless.

And think of the glorious history of this type of punishment compared with others! Think of the heroic spies who did valiant service for their country, only to be apprehended in the end. Think of the emperors, kings, and noblemen of the past and present, subversive leaders, and others who achieved mortality and were courageous enough to look death squarely in the eye and refused to wear an eye band.

Alas, this option is not available in many states. You may have to settle for the electric chair, the gas chamber, or in truly advanced states, lethal injections.

Whether you were able to identify with the condemned murderer in choosing the method that is to end his or her life, or whether you were not, all the choices in one way or another are uncivilized, primitive, barbaric, and cruel. It is doubtful that a human way of deliberately terminating a human life can ever be found.

It appears that execution per se, and modes of execution, can never replace God's way—fate's way—of ending life. In fact, it is one of the merciful aspects of human existence that we do not know the moment when we will leave that existence. Society's way of determining the precise hour when and method by which a killer-victim will die takes out of God's hands what is God's decision only.

To summarize: advocates of the death penalty present roughly the following argument on the subject of inherent cruelty: 1) The killer-victim committed a murder—an act of cruelty. 2) Therefore, it is moral to send him or her to death—admittedly also an act of cruelty. 3) By seeking to reduce the level of cruelty, i.e., by finding humane ways of terminating a guilty life, we have done our human duty. 4) There is no other appropriately severe punishment that fits the crime of murder.

Opponents of the death penalty argue, on the subject of cruelty, that 1) The killer-victim committed a murder—an act of cruelty. 2) It does not follow that society in turn should commit an act of cruelty by dispatching him or her to death. 3) There is no humane way to execute—only ways of varying cruelty. 4) An alternative form of punishment exists—mandatory life imprisonment—that does not taint society with brutality, cruelty, or execution.

Clearly, the advocates of capital punishment are horrified mainly by the cruelty of the initial murder.

Just as clearly, the opponents are also horrified by the cruelty of the initial murder, but they are horrified by the cruelty of the state when it executes a live human being as well.

The question then becomes: Who is revolted more by the initial murder, and who is also revolted by the alleged murder of the state? Advocates say that had the initial murder not taken place, there would have been no need for the subsequent act—but this may beg the question.

We all have different values, and we all see cruelty, executions, and methods of execution in different contexts. We can play games of logic with both positions that lead to validity but not necessarily to a meaningful, acceptable truth. Whether the death penalty per se is cruel, barbaric, and inhuman must be weighed on the scale of moral values that, we hope, mature adults have in their possession.

7

Racial Discrimination

Never suffer the prejudice of the eye to determine the heart.
— J. G. Zimmermann

O N March 25, 1931, nine young men, all of them black, were
jailed in Alabama, charged with raping two white girls. Seldom in U.S. history has a case produced comparable feelings of racial hatred. Only the greatest effort by the authorities averted a
lynching.

In the trial that followed, the accused were without benefit of
counsel. The jury was all white. The most primitive expressions of
racial prejudice were heard and to all intents and purposes tolerated.
With the exception of one, all the accused were found guilty and
sentenced to die in the electric chair.

It is widely believed that the sentence would have been carried
out but for the intervention of outside groups. Organizations like the
International Labor Council carried out protests, provided counsel,
and tirelessly demanded justice for the black men. Protests were
heard from as far away as Europe and from as close by as large cities
outside the South. Pressure mounted steadily for reconsideration of
the case. The combined efforts of northern politicians and distinguished jurists and the notoriety the case received in the press helped
bring the matter before the U.S. Supreme Court. Toward the end
of 1932 the Court overturned the convictions of seven of the men,
and a new trial was ordered. Sometime into the new trial, one of the
"raped victims" reneged on her testimony, admitting she had perjured herself.

Thus, all the men, known as the Scottsboro boys, escaped the electric chair. Still, there was damage to their lives. They suffered profound anguish and loss of reputation. The prison time they served left a big gap in their lives.

Could the story of the Scottsboro boys be repeated, even after black Americans have gained so many civil and legal rights?

In his *Furman* opinion, Justice Powell declared that the racial segregation in American society of decades past, "which contributed substantially to the severity of punishment for interracial crimes, is now no longer prevalent in this country."[1]

This statement seemed less absurd in 1972, after the civil rights efforts of the Johnson administration, than it does today. When Justice Powell expressed his optimistic view, there was hope of further reducing segregation, but this hope has hardly been fulfilled. Segregation has diminished in many areas in the South; yet de facto segregation continues on the whole, particularly in the metropolitan areas of the North and Northeast.

In his opinion for the same case, Justice William O. Douglas (quoting former attorney general Ramsey Clark) asserted that, now as before, the death penalty has been reserved for the poor, the weak, the powerless.[2] Justice Marshall, himself a member of a minority, maintained that if most citizens were aware "of the disproportionate infliction of the death penalty on the poor, the ignorant and the underprivileged, they would suffer a shock to their conscience and sense of justice."[3] Both justices' statements should be taken not at face value but as an admonition on the part of one and an expression of hope on the part of the other.

The racial dilemma is considerable. It is a fact that over half of those accused of murder are black; but over half of the victims are also black. As one logician puts it, if black murderers are not severely punished, what value does this attach to the lives of their black victims?

Black intellectuals have been troubled by the inability of accused members of their race to mount adequate legal defenses. But ghetto blacks themselves may be more concerned about their own safety in the face of increasing crime than defending black accused killers. It is not likely that problematic procedural questions or the lack of top-notch defense lawyers is uppermost on the ghetto-dweller's mind. As a law-abiding citizen, the ghetto resident is more likely to identify with the victim of a crime than with the color of the criminal. If anything, he or she has more cause to feel retributive toward the black killer, given the fact that it is other blacks who are more often than not the victims of black killers.

Blacks and some other minorities are the have-nots in America. Like have-nots in all societies, they are subject to greater pressure and temptation to commit crimes than better-off citizens are. Justice Powell correctly dubbed this a tragic by-product of social and economic deprivation.[4]

Poverty-stricken minorities are especially prone to become involved in crime in an age in which drugs are all too often the answer to despair. Drugs make one "feel good" about oneself and the world. But the moment the effect of the drug wears off, the darkness of an existence without compensation or hope can plunge one into renewed despair; only a new dose of the drug can restore the desire even to live. Drugs are illegal and expensive, and to their users they seem necessary to survival. Individuals in such desperate straits will do anything to secure this necessity, and once in a while, doing so will lead to crime. And so it often happens that the vicious circle of poverty, hopelessness, and despair lands minority youngsters in serious trouble with the law, including on occasion the charge of murder. When this happens, the minority convict undergoes a double penalty: society has created the circumstances leading to his desolation and despair, and society now punishes him for what that desolation and despair have led to. The values that most middle-class Americans were taught are values that such youngsters have neither learned nor appreciate. They are clearly values for the haves, not the have-nots—the group to which many minorities see themselves permanently relegated. Blamed by society for not being able to get jobs, distrusted for "not wanting to work," and sometimes automatically suspected because of their color, black youngsters get questioned by police ahead of anyone else, when anything goes amiss. Because of the higher incidence of violent crime and criminal penalties among minorities, and because of economic barriers and other social evils, should a society demonstrate greater leniency toward black criminals? Hardly! We cannot lose sight of the fundamental principles of American justice, the government's responsibility to protect citizens and, in this case especially, the many black victims of crime. At the

same time, we must make absolutely certain that the black criminals—including murderers—do not suffer discrimination because of
their color.

In some respects, the lot of the black murder suspect has improved in recent years. All-white juries in murder cases involving
blacks have become rare. Prejudice may still exist in the jury room;
perhaps it has become even more stubborn since it has had to cam-
ouflage itself. But the majority of Americans attempt to meet the
challenge of fairness when put to the test. Others may have to sub-
limate their negative feelings about a minority group. It was a sign
that better times had arrived when in a new post–*Furman* statute,
Georgia authorized its supreme court to set aside a death sentence if
it had been handed down as a result of prejudice and passion on the
part of either the judge or jury. This statute is encouraging in view
of the fact that between 1930 and 1982, Georgia executed the most
persons of any state, and well over half of them were black.[5] Even if
more blacks were involved in violent crimes there, it seems unthink-
able that race was not a convicting factor. Race may still be a factor
in American courtrooms, if not in Georgia's. In the fall of 1988, the
National Coalition to Abolish the Death Penalty studied death row
inmates and classified them according to the racial-ethnic categories
White, Black, Hispanic, Native American, Asian, and Unknown.
Their study reveals some interesting—and depressing—statistics.
Large numbers of blacks are found on the death rows of mostly non-
southern states, except for Texas (102) and Florida (101)—and the
latter can hardly be considered a southern state in any but a geo-
graphical sense. For example, there were 87 in California, 74 in Il-
linois, 45 in Ohio, and 53 in Pennsylvania.[6] The total number of
blacks on the various death rows was 855, and whites, 1,094. Even
when one adds to the latter figure the number of Hispanics plus
Unknowns—127—blacks still represent a startling 70 percent. One
must wonder whether the fact that blacks are involved in more violent crimes accounts for such a high percentage. The proportion of
blacks to whites who have actually been executed since 1976 (as opposed to the proportion of death row inmates) is not as inflated;
there, the numbers are less skewed. According to a report of August
1, 1988, of the Legal Defense Fund of the NAACP, only 101 persons
have been executed, of whom 39 were black (38.61 percent) and 56

were white (55.45 percent). Of the murderers' victims, 11 were black (10.89 percent) and 87 were white (86.13 percent).

Though the secrecy of jury room deliberations offers some safeguards against traditional social and ethnic bigotry, this does not necessarily mean that an accused black will always receive a fair trial. Nowadays this problem is linked as much to the prevalence of black people's poverty in this country as to their color.

How and where, for example, can a black person accused of murder hope to find a lawyer of quality? Lawyers with skill in trial work can command fees of from $500 to $1,200 a day. The accused will also want and need an investigator, who will claim a sizable fee of his or her own, and the accused may need high-priced psychiatrists and psychologists to testify as well. The chances of a poor person's receiving the services of such personnel seem less than bright. Court-appointed attorneys, often fresh out of law school, hardly have the experience needed to handle capital offenses and give clear direction to an investigation.

Suppose we look at a hypothetical case. A black man of ghetto origin is accused of stabbing a man. He claims that the stabbing occurred in self-defense, after he had struggled with his victim. Clearly, he will need a capable attorney from the first moment, and almost as soon, an investigator to follow several trails. To whom did the murder weapon belong? Who bought it—and when and where? What was the history of the dead man? Did he have any criminal record? Is there any evidence that the victim committed a previous assault or previously used a knife or other weapon? Whatever evidence can be uncovered through careful research about the dead man's past could strengthen the case for assault on his part and self-defense on the part of the accused and is valid and necessary for the defense.

The investigator must also look into the background of the accused. Has he ever pulled a knife on anyone, or threatened another person? What witnesses can testify to his character and social behavior?

What about the weapon? If it was not found by the police, has anyone made an adequate attempt to locate it? Or have all parties assumed, all too easily, that they have an open-and-shut case and that they have a likely murderer, and thus made only halfhearted attempts to locate the weapon? If the crime was committed recently, only a day or two before, the investigator and his helpers could still find the weapon.

But it is difficult for a black defendant to marshal the resources to hire a first-rate investigator. The assigned lawyer and his budget will hardly permit this. The result is that his defense may well seem doomed from the first, and this may lead the lawyer to recommend, in the absence of needed proof, a guilty plea to a lesser charge, if the prosecutor is so inclined. If this effort fails, an almost certain verdict of guilty—possibly for first-degree murder—is likely.

The accused can be of some help in his own defense; normally, he can give the court-appointed attorney some leads. All too often, however, the accused is poorly educated and insufficiently articulate to provide his attorney with the ideas, suggestions, and even clues that the lawyer needs to proceed effectively on his own.

Suppose that a valid case for self-defense could not be established and that the defendant has been found guilty of murder in the first degree. A separate sentence hearing now generally follows the convictions. Can any mitigating circumstances be found that would result in a sentence other than death? Here again, the court-assigned attorney, less experienced and often less able, can do less for the convicted person than a lawyer who is thoroughly experienced in capital cases and who is able to cast the defendant in a light that the jury would not otherwise see. Of course, our imaginary poor black defendant may be guilty—irredeemably guilty, and irredeemable, period, with nothing to protect him from the maximal penalty. But the question still remains: did he receive the best possible defense under the circumstances? Or was he prevented from doing so by poverty? In this case, there was clearly "class justice"—the defendant, of below-average ability to help himself, was given an attorney of below-average ability and had inadequate resources to carry it all out.

Thus, an accused black person, coming from a statistically proven environment of relatively high crime rates, is arrested by officers of the law who are aware of his or her origin, who are distrustful of his background, who are biased to believe in his guilt, and who are under pressure to see to it that he is incapacitated, preferably by means of a sentence of death. In addition, he has difficulties in presenting the best possible defense under the circumstances.

It is true that people of means experience less pressure to commit violent crimes and in fact do commit fewer, not only absolutely but also relatively. But still there have been murders at the highest levels of society—often willful, gratuitous, and brutal ones. People at those levels have also been the victims of such murders. But with high-priced defense teams at their command, few upper-class murderers have been executed or even given life terms. No wonder the late Justice Douglas wrote that "one searches in vain for the execution of any member of the affluent strata of society."[7] Clinton Duffy, a former warden at San Quentin, agrees: "The death penalty is a privilege of the poor."[8]

Blacks at present constitute around 15 percent of the U.S. population—up from the 10 percent of the last half century—but they constitute a little over 40 percent of the inhabitants of death row. Evidence of continuing racial discrimination is disturbing, especially given the safeguards against arbitrariness and discrimination built into the judicial machinery. Moreover, other facts are also unsettling[9]:

- White convicts' sentences are commuted more often than those of blacks convicted of capital crimes. One Pennsylvania study singles out race as the sole distinguishing factor.

- Where rape is the crime for which the convict is executed, 90 percent are black. It is significant that no white man has ever been executed for raping a black woman.

- In Ohio between 1974 and 1977, 173 black men killed white persons. Twenty-five percent of these murderers were given the death penalty. During the same period, forty-seven white men killed black men, but not one was sentenced to die.

- Over roughly the same period in Florida, 842 blacks killed whites; 126 were sentenced to die. Two hundred ninety-four whites killed blacks; but only three received the death penalty.

It is evident that the changes brought about in the wake of *Furman* have not removed the two-tiered system of justice for capital crimes. And yet one might have expected that relatively more attention would be given to the problem of discrimination in sentencing, given the cautions and admonitions of the Supreme Court. A 1975 quantitative study by William Bowers and Glenn Pierce came to a shocking conclusion: that systematic discrimination based on race in the judicial process often led to a death sentence.[10]

The Bowers-Pierce study focused on the new sentencing statutes that were applied during part of the moratorium period in Florida, Georgia, Texas, and Ohio (the first three states having a strong history upholding the death penalty). The investigators reported that these states tended to sentence most harshly when the murderer was black and when the victim was white. In other words, a far higher premium was placed on the life of a white murderer than on the life of a black murderer; similarly, a lower premium was placed on the black victim than on the white victim. A black life continues to have less value in the sentencing process, despite Justice Powell's optimistic 1972 assessment.[11]

In 173 cases of blacks killing whites, 44 death sentences were imposed, roughly one-quarter of the time.

Where a white man killed a white man (in 803 cases in all), only 37 death sentences were inflicted, less than 5 percent of the time.

Where blacks killed blacks—the highest incidence, 1170 cases—only 20 death sentences were handed down, for less than one-fifth of 1 percent.

Where whites killed blacks—47 cases—not a single death sentence was recorded.

Obviously, judges and juries do not look upon the killing of a black man with the same disapproval with which they regard the killing of a white man, be it by a black or white. A black killing a white is judged a far more serious crime than a black killing another black. A white killing a black is forgiven far more readily than a white killing another white. The act that seems to be most deserving of retribution, to be dealt with most harshly, is the killing of a white by a black. The addition of a sexual element—if the black man's victim is a white woman—produces the ultimate and most unforgivable sin.[12]

These statistics alone should probably force the authorities who enacted the post–*Furman* statutes to examine whether the nondiscriminatory goals have been met. Discrimination that leads to permanent imprisonment is severe enough. But discrimination that leads to execution ranges somewhere between the harsh and the intolerable. No law leading to discriminatory results is likely to be constitutional; yet it is doubtful that any fairer doctrines can be enunciated than those now in existence.

Those "mitigating circumstances" instituted in the post–*Furman* world to protect convicts from the death penalty do not seem to have achieved the purpose for which they were set up, all good intentions notwithstanding. Similarly, the "aggravating circumstances" do not seem to have led to the results envisaged by the post–*Furman* judges.

In *Gregg v. Georgia*, 1976, the most important post–*Furman* decision, the Supreme Court addressed the adequacy of guidelines available to judges and juries. The Court did not address the role of the prosecutors who determine which criminal case calls for the death penalty and which does not. Prosecutors are judged by their conviction records, and blacks are ostensibly easier to convict than whites. The relationship between this prosecutorial option and the discrimination revealed by the Bower and Pierce study are not difficult to fathom.

Because executions are rare, many observers have called the use of the death penalty a symbolic act to indicate society's desire for justice. But the death penalty may actually be used for another purpose: to find a scapegoat for society's inability to deal with crime— and that scapegoat may be the black man. Perhaps he is also the scapegoat for many social ills today: so many blacks unemployed, so many on the welfare rolls, so many with illegitimate children at a deplorable age, so many involved in drug abuse.

Some feel that no legal standards can be devised that could overcome the social inequities that cause blacks to commit a larger proportion of crimes and to receive a large proportion of death sentences and executions. Realistic observers of humankind know that racial problems cannot be legislated away. Hans Zeisel thinks that the very fact that a defendant's race sometimes affects sentencing is sufficient reason to abolish capital punishment. He weakens his own argument, however, when he admits that prosecutors are much more in control than jurors and thus could markedly reduce discrimination without our throwing out the death penalty altogether.[13]

The changes that occurred in the wake of *Furman*, while surely representing an advance in overcoming arbitrariness and discrimination, are still in some measure cosmetic. The Supreme Court can say in good faith that it has sought to combat the inequities; politicians can make a comparable claim. They have all indeed done something, but whether that something amounts to anything substantial remains questionable. There is simply too much underlying racial prejudice and too much social and economic inequality for either to be eradicated at the several crucial levels at which they appear.

Should we then throw up our hands in despair and assume that nothing can be done? That would hardly be just or expedient. Murderers, whether black or white, must receive the harshest penalty that an enlightened and just society can impose. This is in the interest of the total society, as well as of the decent, law-abiding black citizens who are the primary victims of murderers. But whether this penalty should be another killing, given the special circumstances surrounding blacks in particular, is another question altogether.

8

Retributive Justice

Life is a comedy to him who thinks and a tragedy to him
who feels.

— Horace Walpole

O PPONENTS of the death penalty regard the deliberate, planned termination of a fully developed human life as cruel and as intrinsically barbaric as the tools of execution themselves. They regard one rationale given for executing a human being as only slightly less barbaric: humankind's desire for vengeance, for getting even, for making sure the killer gets his or her just deserts. Revenge strikes the abolitionist as an uncivilized, primitive, cruel, debasing, and shameful motive for execution.

Though proponents of capital punishment do not equate retribution, the appropriate reward for good or evil, with vengeance, the infliction of punishment, often excessive, in return for an injury, they acknowledge that retribution cannot be entirely divorced from revenge. Retentionists see revenge as an entirely natural emotion and necessary to maintain the basic social order. Before legalized retribution had fully developed, as in the American West, they argue, lynchings were used to ensure that society's need for the criminal to "pay up" was satisfied. More concerned with the interests of the victim than with those of the murderer, retentionists see retribution as an eminently fair approach to justice.

The other day a friend complained to one of the authors that his minister was not in the habit of returning phone calls, yet the latter wanted his parishioners to respond at once when he contacted *them*. The parishioner felt snubbed that the minister had not returned one of his calls. He vowed he would not take the minister's call the next time. Why not? "It satisfies me," he said with a smile.

Similarly, someone who returns home from a Sunday-afternoon outing and finds that his home has been invaded by burglars who took only insignificant belongings nonetheless wants the police to apprehend the burglars and expects the judicial system to make sure they land behind bars. To some extent, the resentment stems from the desire to get even, to see punishment inflicted where punishment traditionally is due. It is also linked to deterrence in that the home-owner would like to spare others the anguish of being burglarized. The same feelings obtain when we are mugged, our persons at-tacked, our intimate personal possessions stolen.

In fact, we do not need to experience these criminal activities personally to become aroused. When we read of crimes happening on our street, or on a street known to us, or to a person with whom we are acquainted even vaguely, similar resentments arise in us, if perhaps a trifle less vigorously. The closer the victim is to us person-ally, or the more we can comprehend and identify with the victim, the more we are inclined to demand that a penalty suitable to the crime be imposed.

Obviously, the only penalty perceived as just for murder, the most serious of human offenses, is the one that claims the life of the murderer. The phrase "an eye for an eye," the *lex talionis*, most effec-tively symbolizes the retributive demand. When the crime is mur-der, this actually translates to "a life for a life"—however dreadful may be for some the notion of putting an end to a breathing human life. At first glance, punishment equal to the damage done seems unambiguous and devoid of vengeance. The trouble is, the precision demanded by the *lex talionis* is not easily arrived at. Qualitative re-tribution must be joined to quantitative retribution and express both a minimum and a maximum punishment, else the "*talio* principle" is not precisely served.

For those who believe that retribution is still the most just all-around punishment, anything less than the death penalty for the crime of murder diminishes the severity of that crime and thereby devalues life. It is likely that the desire for retribution, even more than deterrence, is at the root of the popular clamor for the death penalty. Clearly with that idea in mind, Justice Thurgood Marshall insisted that the death penalty cannot have validity unless it is based on "informed public opinion" (as opposed to mere public opinion) and not on retributive justice.[1] Retribution, as Marshall and other abolitionists see it, is primitive and was suited to the justices of primitive times, not to those of our enlightened era.

Justice Harry Blackmun believes that public opinion should be heeded: "[The] elected representatives of the people [are] far more conscious of the temper of the times, of the maturing of society, and the contemporary demands for man's dignity than are we who sit cloistered in this Court."[2] Justice Brennan agrees with Justice Blackmun that majority opinion should be heeded and concludes that it has been, for so few persons have lately been executed. Blackmun's answer is that the infrequent imposition of a particular penalty implies not that the public rejects that penalty but that it reserves its use for "a small number of cases." As Chief Justice Burger asserts, "If selective imposition evidences a rejection of capital punishment in those cases where it is not imposed, it surely evidences a correlative affirmation of the penalty in those cases where it is imposed."[3]

Penologists, who believe in rehabilitating prisoners and returning them to society cured of their malady—admittedly, a fond hope—have objected to retributive justice in lesser penalties than the death penalty. Yet the waves of crime in our drug-infested, rootless society have rendered them relatively silent on the matter of the death penalty. They have largely allowed the principle to stand that a punishment should be proportionate to the type of crime committed. But on the subject of murder they draw the line on this principle, as it has been interpreted in the past. For anti–death penalty penologists, the penalty of life imprisonment—permanent, irrevocable confinement—fits the crime of murder as well as execution does. Alone among all types of punishment, death cannot be recalled, revoked, altered, or made more or less severe. Because of its finality, the death penalty seems to many unnecessary and excessive when murderers can be segregated by society, prevented from committing further deeds, and suffer the severest punishment that society can inflict—without society itself becoming indirectly a murderer.

If the penalty of life imprisonment were truly for life, many retentionists might well be converted to the abolitionist cause. But in reality, very few people die a natural death in prison. Their all-too-early reappearance on the street explains in large measure the hard-line attitude of many concerned citizens about the death penalty. In his lecture entitled "Concessions to Retribution in Punishment" delivered first in 1978, Hugo Adam Bedau posits, for purposes of argument, a just society of moral, rational members against which, because of its justness, there is little reason or justification to commit a crime. In addition, there is maximum freedom for all in this society. This society has no need for punishment because there is no crime. Such a society, argues Bedau, is obviously an ideal—and one worth striving for. But to the extent the present society deviates from this ideal, it has a right to demand compliance with the ideal. The penalty for noncompliance is loss of freedom—i.e., the forfeiture of the equal rights one shares with other members of society—not death.

Proponents and opponents of capital punishment probably concur that there is an element of revenge in retributive justice—maybe the largest element in it—and that it may indeed be the reason for the masses' continued support for the death penalty. Revenge has surely been a permanent fixture on the scene of human emotions; it releases pent-up anger and frustrations. But in the matter of the death penalty, revenge is a dangerous and destructive—even if understandably human—reaction.

Again and again in newspaper accounts of murder trials, relatives of murder victims express deep frustration and anger at the very notion that the admitted killers have any defense at all. They are impatient with the legal process and its built-in guarantees that ensure a fair trial for the accused. Invariably, they feel cheated when the verdict is less than guilty—even if the evidence is clearly insufficient to convict—or, when convicted, the accused is given a sentence less than death. The brothers, sisters, and parents of the murder victim sit through trial sessions day after day and are highly vocal in expressing their impatience and dissatisfaction if there is even a respite for the killer, whether due to a mistrial or to a technicality. After all, they feel, they have suffered the ultimate loss, and they demand a corresponding loss for whoever caused theirs.

Yet although their attitude is human, it is hardly elevating or in line with the nobler trends of religious faith. Also, while the desire for retribution is understandable for individuals, it is hardly so for groups. People of a particular ethnic, religious, or racial group sometimes agitate for the death of a criminal belonging to another such group—see the lynchings and the white justice in alleged rape cases in both true-life and fictional accounts. (Richard Wright's *Native Son* is a case in point.) That they do so is not surprising, but it is often difficult to fathom. Group desire for revenge for a wrong done, whether real or imagined, lacks both the innocence and the purity of the desire for vengeance felt by the individual.

Even on the individual level, however, revenge remains a primitive, animalistic response, however natural. The Bible, although replete with examples of vengeance, repeats the admonition of the divinity, "Thou shalt not take vengeance nor bear a grudge." The Lord makes it clear that vengeance is His, "as well as recompense." "Leave to God the avenging," we are told in the Apocrypha, as well as, "Requite not evil to your neighbor for any wrong."

Great secular thinkers have also doubted the ethics and nobility of revenge as a catalyst for human action and justice. Seneca, in the Roman Empire, called *revenge* "an inhuman word"; at about the same time, Marc Antony wrote that the best sort of revenge is to be different from him who did the injury. Sir Francis Bacon dubbed *revenge* a kind of wild justice. Percy Bysshe Shelley's unequivocal condemnation holds special significance for the death penalty: "Revenge is the naked idol of the worship of a semi-barbarous age."

But there have also been others who held the opposite view. The best-known philosophers to support the notion of retribution are Kant and Hegel. Kant saw punishment as an end in itself, not as a means to some good for individual or society. Hegel maintained that the criminal has a right to retribution, that punishment is as good and necessary for the criminal as it is for society. Since it does not appear that the world is metaphysically ordered in such a way as to ensure that punishment always follows evil deeds, humans must create their own moral order.

As thoughtful a student of the death penalty as Walter Berns has called its retention desirable because it keeps a people angry enough to defend the sanctity of life. Berns, however, may be guilty of three errors or near errors: for he forgets that anger leads to passion, that passion leads to fanaticism, and that fanaticism leads to lack of thought and control. An angry, passionate demand for taking someone's life is far uglier than the initial anger generated by homicide. For some, anger generated by homicide is adequately served by a demand for life imprisonment of the murderer, with no chance of parole or reprieve; it also demonstrates respect for the sanctity of life. Berns may be among the few philosophers to celebrate anger as a moral cause.

Retribution may well originate in anger—a feeling that has served all animals throughout time as an effective means of survival. Translating anger into revenge seems to provide a biological foundation for retributive acts, but it certainly does not justify them morally. Its biological connection may explain why some say that retribution is intuitive—that is, it is felt without conscious reasoning; we "know" it inferentially. But although disapproval is felt, the means of implementing that disapproval are not at all clear.

Scripture provides some guidance on anger: it does not value anger highly. We are told in Ecclesiastes 7:9 that "anger rests in the bosom of fools" and in Job 5:2 that "anger kills the foolish man." We are warned not to let the sun go down upon our wrath. Moreover, "He that is slow to anger is better than the mighty; and he that ruleth his spirit, than he that taketh a city." Anger, we are told in the Talmud, "deprives a sage of his wisdom, a prophet of his vision."

Nor have secular thinkers assigned a high value to anger. English novelist Edward Bulwer-Lytton (1831–91) regards it as less desirable than Berns does: "Anger ventilated often hurries toward forgiveness; anger concealed often hardens into revenge." Minot Judson (1841–1918), Unitarian clergyman, also questioned anger: "When anger rushes unrestrained to action, like a hot steed, it stumbles on the way. The man of thought strikes deepest and strikes safely." The American lecturer R. G. Ingersoll (1833–99) agreed: "Anger blows out the lamp of the mind. In the examination of a great and important question, everyone should be serene, slow-pulsed, and calm."

The thinking of others, clearly in the minority, has paralleled Berns's more closely. Richard W. Whately (1787–1863), archbishop of Dublin, completely agreed with him. "Anger," he maintained, "requires that the offender should not only be made to grieve in his turn, but to grieve for that particular wrong which has been done by him."

Some thinkers have praised anger for reasons that may not be acceptable to conservatives like Professor Berns. Liberals judge anger to be at the base of "consciousness raising" and crucial to an awareness of social evils. Without anger, liberals claim, there can be no real progress: poverty will remain poverty, slums will remain slums, hunger will remain hunger, and inadequate health care will remain just that. Although here, too, anger leads to passion and fanaticism, these are galvanized into social action. In a democracy, social action is theoretically limited to peaceful demonstrations, to political activism, and to pleading and demanding with the powers that be. In less stable societies, the same anger, if not satisfied, may lead to the very revolutions that Professor Berns would surely abhor. Anger is thus a two-edged sword, and from the standpoint of any moderate, it had better be kept under strict surveillance.

In his defense of anger and retribution, Professor Berns finds evidence in the Old Testament that supports the death penalty. When God speaks against revenge—and presumably the anger behind it—Berns tells us He is speaking to the individual human being; when He speaks in favor of retribution, He is addressing the legal community. This distinction between the desirability of restraining the individual human being and the need to punish criminals severely and collectively for the community is interesting, but why couldn't it have been the other way around, or why couldn't God have addressed the individual and the legal community at the same time? For example, Berns tells us, God was addressing the legal community when He said, "And he that killeth any man shall surely be put to death" (Exod. 21:12). This could also mean that the Divinity will see to it Himself that the murderer is put to death. And again, when God says, "Ye shall take no satisfaction [meaning ransom] for the life of a murderer, which is guilty of death, but he shall surely be put to death," Berns views it as an argument for the death penalty. But it could also in fact be a warning against it, an assertion that punishment by death is God's province and His alone. For God makes this ultimate admonition to men and women both as individuals and as social beings: "Thou shalt not kill" (Exod. 20:13).

Proponents of the death penalty often complain that abolitionists neglect the memory of the murder victim in favor of seeking to defend the perpetrator of homicide, favoring, as it were, Cain over Abel. This is not usually and certainly not necessarily so. If Scripture teaches that Cain as well as Abel is made in the image of God, this does not mean that Cain and Abel are equally deserving. Abolitionists hold that because Cain is the slayer and Abel his victim, Cain should be banished, exiled, or segregated; he should become worse than a pariah in the eyes of society. In fact, God must protect him from the wrath of others who would take his life in retribution. Cain has become execrable because he murdered his brother, but people may not kill him. The community must rather isolate him permanently to make certain that he will not kill again. Only God may do away with him in His own good time.

This is the view not only of some religiously oriented abolitionists as well as secularist abolitionists; other religious persons argue that it is the evil act that is condemnable, not the person. But because it is the person who symbolizes and has performed the deed, he or she inevitably is condemned by society. Therefore, these abolitionists argue, it is essential to weigh the good and the bad in people who have committed heinous crimes, to assess the total character of the human being, and perhaps to find some mitigating fact or circumstances that enable society to inflict a penalty less harsh and less self-incriminating than the death penalty.

Of course, most religious people in the Western nations today are religious more in name than in spirit or deed. They do not feel they have to obey scripture literally. Hence, biblical evidence is not the guiding light for most people, except where religious teachings are so deeply embedded that they direct human behavior from the recesses of consciousness. Like most rational people, they will consider questions like deterrence and retribution calmly, weighing the evidence; when they are less than rational, red-hot anger, emotional reactions, and the desire for quick and ruthless justice will determine their choices.

Gallup polls and the results of the 1988 presidential election (in which the death penalty was one of the major issues) all suggest that the "guts" approach prevails in the present United States, with its rising crime rates. It is for this reason that Justice Marshall drew his distinction between *public opinion* and *informed public opinion*. Yet not even familiarity with the laws of the various states, statistics on people executed, and the debates in our judicial system are likely to affect popular attitudes toward executions when headlines and television broadcasts showing brutal crimes raise our blood to the boiling point. Undoubtedly, Justice Marshall had in mind informed and thoughtful opinion, in which the rational in people is fused with the emotional.

It is reasonable to assume that Justice Marshall knows the statistics concerning public approval of the death penalty. His insistence on informed—i.e., rational—opinion may also have been stimulated by the fact that 8 or more percent of voters are willing to endorse the death penalty for robbers and muggers. Such an excessive penalty for lesser crimes could indeed serve as a deterrent, but it would also violate the principle of retributive, proportional justice. There can be no doubt that these 8 percent are expressing their legitimate anger at crime, the insecurity they feel in walking the streets, and their fears of having their homes invaded. But many supporters of capital punishment were also motivated by tradition or by loyalty to a beloved public leader—such as President Reagan—as well as by assumptions about deterrence and retribution.

In a democracy, public opinion has to be considered on all issues. But there is some doubt that undifferentiated public opinion ought to play a role when it comes to the question of extinguishing a human life, degraded though that life may be. The idea of "informed opinion" remains a bit vague; the Court's support for a public opinion "which is enlightened by human justice" may have to do for the foreseeable future. (Admittedly, this approach is hard to square with selection of jurors undifferentiated except by challenges.)

Empirical studies of opponents and proponents of the death penalty have found that each tends toward certain political affiliations and to have a certain personality type. Abolitionists are more likely to be found left of the political center, in the peace camp, environmentalist groups, on the antimilitarist side; they are also likely to support an extension of public education and the notion of nonmilitary service to the nation. They tend to be outside the mainstream of current American life, dismissible as do-gooders or starry-eyed dreamers. As personality types, they tend to be less well-organized, to be unsystematic in approach, to be attracted to the new and less respectful of what has been and to be more cynical regarding officialdom.

Retentionists are generally more conservative. They tend to view the military more favorably, to assign a lower priority to the plight of so-called oppressed groups, and to oppose many social benefits to those who have not earned them. In matters of life and death, they tend to favor freedom from gun control and tight restrictions on abortions. Personality studies depict them as dogmatic, relatively authoritarian, and more prone to restrict civil liberties.

There are surely also hard-headed realists among the abolitionists and thoughtful, open-minded individuals among the retention-ists. Yet to dismiss these empirical portraits as worthless would be as foolish as to accept them without reservations. More than a grain of truth exists in the conviction that more realists than dreamers support retributive justice. The truth is that the question of the justice of retribution is likely to be discussed in terms of values and philosophy rather than in carefully structured scientific studies.

Retributive justice can become a dangerous, destructive, and totally unfair form of justice when it is linked to racism—a force that is hardly diminishing on our social scene (see chapter 6). As Justice Douglas declared in his *Furman* opinion, death sentences have traditionally been imposed and carried out in disproportionate numbers on "the poor, the Negro, and the members of unpopular groups." In some border and southern states, blacks have been punished especially harshly for raping white females. Given the horror with which interracial sexual relations are regarded in many parts of the country, the rape and murder of a white woman by a black man are likely to arouse the kind of desire for instant justice and revenge that demands the death of the black man. Rape of a black woman by a white man has never reached that blood-boiling point of vengeance in the white community. But it is becoming an issue of vital concern in the black community.

It is not only rape, however, that galvanizes calls for retribution. Statistics suggest that poverty, drug infestation, less-than-adequate housing, and family conditions in the inner city have produced far higher levels of crime there than elsewhere. Though whites are victims of crime more rarely than blacks, recurring stories of black crime—and the incapacity of the black community to respond adequately or powerfully—have created a climate in which demands for the death of "human trash" have become ever more vocal. Thus, the most common object of retribution is being further victimized—a seemingly endless process.

In summary, Lawrence Kohlberg and Donald Elfenbein may well be right in claiming that it is retribution that has traditionally provided the major justification for capital punishment and that only if individual moral judgment shifts away from retribution will the death penalty be perceived as cruel and unusual.[4]

9

Executing the Innocent:
How Great the Risk?

What is our innocence, what is our guilt? All are naked, none is
safe.

— Marianne Moore

I N 1984 the CBS program "60 Minutes" reported the story of a
twenty-six-year-old black engineer who lived in a small Texas
town northeast of Dallas. In 1983, Lenell Geter was identified as the
culprit in a restaurant holdup on the basis of the photo on his driver's
license, and he was arrested for armed robbery. Evidence that Geter
was actually at work while the robbery was occurring made it difficult at first to proceed with the prosecution.

How had Lenell Geter, gainfully employed in a defense plant,
come under suspicion in the first place? It seems that his dangerous
habit of reading and feeding the ducks in a park every day had struck
an elderly lady as suspicious. When she learned that the restaurant
had been held up in August 1983, she informed the police of her
suspicions. The robbery witnesses declared categorically that he was
not the robber—one of the witnesses knew Geter personally. But the
police felt obliged to follow through on the citizen's suspicions and
passed Geter's photo on to police in surrounding towns where similar
holdups had been reported. In one of these towns, Geter was identified as the culprit in at least two robberies. One robbery had netted
the criminal $615. Geter was prosecuted and convicted.

The jury that convicted him was all white. At the sentence hearing, the jury heard that the police chief in his hometown in South

Carolina had called him an outlaw, a statement later denied by the chief. Geter had no previous record. He was sentenced to a life term, of which the minimum time that had to be served was twenty years.

One reason this happened was that Geter's defense was inadequate. The lawyer he had hired abandoned the case once Geter ran out of money. His court-assigned attorney assumed he was guilty and sought to persuade him to plea-bargain. The same lawyer missed the date for filing a petition for a retrial after it became clear that Geter might be the subject of a serious judicial error. Geter was saved from decades of prison only by the intervention of outside groups. Civil rights organizations—mainly the NAACP—provided him with a new, capable, and committed lawyer. Fellow white engineers at Geter's plant raised $11,000 toward his defense fund. After the media, including "60 Minutes," took an interest in the case, the evidence received further scrutiny. It simply did not hold up— which did not prevent the prosecutor from claiming that Geter would be found guilty if another trial were held. Yet, the prosecutor further stated, if Geter should pass a lie-detector test, he would not be tried again. In spite of his belief in Geter's guilt, the prosecutor bent over backward to show that the system is fair and that people should have confidence in it.

The Lenell Geter case does not involve a murder or the death penalty, but it does have many elements—including the sentence— that are characteristic of murder investigations. The errors that were committed here could also have been committed in a capital case: ignorance, prejudice, overly eager police and prosecutor, a false identification, unwillingness to hear all the evidence, unwillingness to reconsider the case, and the need for outside forces to set judicial revision in motion. Luckily, Geter is now free—thanks to CBS more than to our justice system.

More recently, a Texas judge recommended that Randall Dale Adams, who had been convicted for murder, be given a new trial. He had already served twelve years in prison for the shooting of police officer Robert Wood in 1976. All along he had maintained his innocence, claiming that the chief witness had done the shooting. Here again, it was not the judicial authorities that initiated the reexamination of evidence, but the documentary movie *The Thin Blue Line*. In March 1989, an appellate court threw out his conviction.

 Further back in the past, in 1963, two blacks, Pitts and Lee, were sentenced to death after local authorities beat them into confessing to a crime they had not committed. They were saved only because the Supreme Court was then considering the matter of capital punishment in general. While awaiting their fate, a white man confessed to the crime. Despite this confession and the fact that the evidence pointed clearly to the white man's guilt, Florida lawmen did not pursue the lead. They were quite content with their "two nigger prisoners." Twelve years later, the governor pardoned the two men. They would not have seen this success, pitiful though it was, if it had not been for the Supreme Court's reconsideration and moratorium of the death penalty.[1]

In another case where the innocent were convicted, four "bikers" were accused of a mutilation slaying in New Mexico. The four men, who were unpleasant and even dangerous-looking members of a motorcycle gang, seemed likely murderers to the local prosecutors, and in spite of flimsy evidence, the prosec   ing their conviction. These four were als   lty moratorium. Another man confessed to the slaying, and his confession was unmistakably truthful—he drew a precise map of the murder scene. With the unhappy consent of the district attorney, the four "bikers" were released.[2]

In these and over a hundred other cases, those wrongfully convicted were almost without exception members of minority groups, poor, poorly educated, inarticulate, and ill-equipped to fend for themselves.

In this century, a certain number of American men and women who were condemned to die have been saved from execution through some last-minute intervention. At least twenty-three persons who were later discovered to be innocent were less fortunate. They did not escape the chair or the gas chamber and died for crimes they had not committed.

The possibility of error is grave enough that many people concerned with the death penalty oppose capital punishment unconditionally for this reason. The prospect of society killing an innocent person is to them an unadulterated horror. Proponents of the death penalty are, of course, also against executing an innocent person.

Two hundred years ago, the Marquis de Lafayette was already so troubled. "I shall ask for the abolition of the punishment of death," he declared, "until I have the infallibility of human judgment presented to me."[3] More recently, former attorney general Ramsey Clark stated that the fear of error causes many to oppose capital punishment "and . . . they should indeed do so."[4] Fortunately, enough precautions are built into our judicial system that error is unlikely in all but the rarest of cases.

But life imprisonment as a penalty for murderers would avoid these rare errors—and still honor the memories of the murder victims. Many abolitionists, who by no means want the memory of the dead forgotten, believe that protecting the living—even murderers—may be more meaningful than doing honor to the dead. The issue of errors in imposing the death penalty has brought out extreme statements from both sides. Some dogmatic abolitionists have said they would welcome an execution of an innocent person if people reacted to it with enough horror to do away with capital punishment once and for all. At the same time, equally doctrinaire retentionists have claimed that even if an innocent person is executed, his or her death will put the fear of God and the Law into criminal hearts, and at least one murder will have been deterred.

Before delving more deeply into the subject of the death penalty and the innocent, let us consider the study by Hugo Bedau and Michael Radelet entitled "Miscarriages of Justice in Potentially Capital Cases," published in 1987 and spanning the period from 1900 to 1980. (In general, the "potentially capital cases" addressed in the study include those that actually resulted in death or those that probably would have except for some fortuitous circumstance: e.g., the verdict was reduced, the sentence was reduced, or the individual was wrongfully convicted in an abolition state.) The study catalogs 350 cases of possible miscarriage of justice (some of which are based on purely subjective judgment of previously proven cases), and of these, 216 have identifiable persons or groups responsible. The investigators drew upon a wide variety of evidence to prove innocence and admit that "every conceivable factor tending to establish innocence" was not present. They allowed that their evidence "may not convince others." The most common sources of errors were, in order of frequency: perjury by witnesses for the prosecution, negligence among various officials, and unintentional errors by various parties such as police and witnesses. Out of the total Bedau and Radelet claimed to discover 139 cases of innocent persons who were sentenced to death since 1900. A total of twenty-three were executed—

all of them before 1943 and ten of them before 1922.[5] But it should be noted that some of these twenty-three included Sacco and Vanzetti and others about whose guilt the courts were not in doubt.

What is one to make of these numbers, given all the qualifications made by the authors themselves? To some proponents of the death penalty, these figures covering nearly nine decades of a century seem small. They believe that these deaths are easily offset by the probable number of crimes that the death penalty "deterred." They reaffirm their faith in the judicial system, which—as they see it—has proved so reliable that it has erred seriously possibly only 139 times and irretrievably only 23 times in the past ninety years. Furthermore, our sentencing must be gaining in accuracy, to judge from our presumed zero mistake rate over the last forty-five years.

Abolitionists interpret these figures differently: They see 139 near-murders by society and 23 actual murders. Even one death, they claim, would be excessive, since it is the function of society to protect citizens, not to kill them. Abolitionists are equally perturbed by the fact that it was generally not the judicial system that uncovered its errors but outsiders, often initially denounced as meddlers. Admittedly, the most frequent source of error-discovery was defense attorneys; however, abolitionists are uncomfortable that the system cannot discover its own deadly, irrevocable errors but needs outside people—and sometimes pure chance—to do so. Yale Professor Charles Black, in his brilliant little volume *Capital Punishment: The Inevitability of Caprice and Mistake*, traces the many possible sources of error in the judicial system from the moment of arrest through arraignment, from the trial through conviction, from the imposition of the death penalty to the death warrant and beyond. Retentionists may well be rightly amazed that the process has not erred more often, considering the many possible sources of error on the road to a murder verdict and an execution. According to Bedau and Radelet, it was largely dubious work by police and prosecutors that led to many of the errors; in rare cases, this meant the actual suppression of evidence or the avoidance of testimony, usually as part of a deal.

Ursula Bentele, in her study "The Death Penalty in Georgia: Still Arbitrary," relates the disturbing case of Jerry Banks.[6] A black man, Banks came upon two dead bodies while he was hunting. Banks walked back to the main road, hailed a car, and asked the driver to report the dead bodies to the police. Barely one month later,

Banks was accused of the murders. Although a neighbor testified that Banks had been at her home when the two men were shot, Banks was tried, convicted, and sentenced to die in 1975.

Oddly, the driver whom Banks had asked to notify the police was never called as a witness, although he had left his name with the police and had declared himself willing to testify. He had testified to the grand jury and had made a statement to the sheriff. But the sheriff and other officers had withheld his name from Banks and his lawyer. It was because of this deliberate suppression of evidence that the Georgia Supreme Court ordered a new trial for Banks in 1976.

In the second trial, Banks was once again convicted and given the death penalty. At this point, two new lawyers discovered a rather obvious fact: the murder weapon could not have been Banks's hunting rifle. The new attorneys also found new witnesses who would testify in Banks's favor. In a third trial, Banks was cleared of all charges against him. But this new life was granted him only after seven years of proximity to the death penalty, of legal wrangling, and of mental anguish.

An inadequate, court-appointed lawyer was to blame, along with the "deliberate or inadvertent" suppression of several pieces of evidence. The fact had never come up during the first two trials that two men, both white, had been seen bitterly haranguing each other shortly before the murder occurred. This and other relevant facts had been reported to the police, but they had ignored the reports and certainly did not pass them on.

One must therefore wonder about the effects of a recent five-to-four Supreme Court decision that the constitutional rights of a defendant are not violated when police officers lose or destroy evidence that could help clear the defendant, unless they acted in "bad faith."[7] Some might see *Youngblood v. Arizona* as another in a recent series of decisions that have granted greater leeway for mistakes by police and prosecutors. Defendants in all criminal cases are entitled to evidence supporting their case; this is doubly crucial in capital cases. But others might insist that nothing has changed: crimes will not be ignored, whether committed by the accused or by law officials. Presumably, defendants will not be let off "on a technicality," and neither will the suppression of evidence be tolerated.

The Court's majority contended that they did not wish to impose on law enforcement officials an absolute duty to "preserve all material that might be of conceivable evidentiary significance in a particular prosecution." In handing down this decision, the Court overturned the judgment of an Arizona appeals court that had concluded, in a case involving sexual assault, that police violate a defendant's right to a fair trial when they "permit the destruction of evidence that could eliminate the defendant as perpetrator."[8]

Justice Blackmun, writing the minority decision, did not rule out the possibility that the police had acted maliciously in the Arizona case. The police had seized a car, examined it, and then dismantled it without giving the victim a chance to identify it.

No one can doubt that most law enforcement officers are honest, decent, sincere people, as intent on ensuring justice as most citizens—and probably more so. Yet an impatient public often unfairly pressures them to produce results, and they may be tempted to remove pieces of evidence so as to enable the police to close a case and a prosecutor to secure a conviction. How easy it is to rationalize that a certain piece of paper is not important, that photographs are as good as the original object, that someone supplying exculpating evidence does not seem trustworthy. The *Youngblood* decision is disturbing enough as a noncapital case; it could one day lead to a wrongfully imposed death penalty in a capital instance. An earlier justice of the Supreme Court, Felix Frankfurter, once wrote that "the balance of conflicting interests must be weighted most heavily in favor of the procedural safeguards of the Bill of Rights."[9] Have both the public and the Court become too impatient?

In fairness to the judicial system, it must be said that its members are grossly underpaid and overworked, if one is to believe a report by the American Bar Association.[10] "As currently funded," the ABA report states, "the criminal justice system cannot provide the quality of justice the public legitimately expects and the people working within the system wish to deliver." The entire system—police, prosecution, criminal defense, courts, and corrections—has been plagued by the drug problem. Effective presentation, either for the state or for the accused, has become virtually impossible due to unprecedented work loads. This state of affairs is deplorable under any circumstances, but it becomes dangerous when a case involving the charge of first-degree murder is rushed.

In their study assessing the sources of wrongful conviction, Bedau and Radelet identified perjury of a prosecution witness as the most frequent.[11] Witnesses sometimes perjured themselves because they themselves had performed the murder. (In a famous 1982 New York case [the *Carter* case], for example, the defendant was convicted mainly on the testimony of his ex-wife, who later confessed to having committed the crime herself.)

Other witnesses gave false testimony because they had somehow been intimidated by the police or prosecutors. One witness was told by the police that they would "blow his brains out" unless he told "the truth." "The truth," of course, was the false testimony the interrogating officer wanted him to give.[12]

The most common reason for perjury, however, was the "prison-inmate deal." In such a deal, someone who is already behind bars and/or is facing serious charges is promised lenient treatment if he or she testifies against the defendant. In Maryland in 1980, David W. Robertson was convicted on two counts of first-degree murder and sentenced to two life terms. He had been present when a friend murdered two innocent persons. This murderer–co-defendant testified falsely against Robertson because the prosecution warned that they would seek the death penalty for him unless he more seriously implicated Robertson. The revelation of perjured testimony led to Robertson's exoneration in 1984. The co-defendant is serving a life term.[13]

Sometimes police acted according to their own perceptions of a suspect. Bedau and Radelet tell us that in the Maryland case police regarded the man who was later exonerated as an evil person who had previously emerged unscathed from other accusations. Since he had managed to "get away with it" before, the police were doubly determined this time not to let it happen again.[14]

The Maryland case is by no means isolated. In Philadelphia in 1983 the prosecution pressured a witness who had reneged on an earlier statement into not testifying. He agreed to it only after he was told he would not be shown leniency on a charge *he* was facing. The result was that only the original incriminating statement was heard, and the inconsistencies in the testimony were lost. Although the accused in the case was charged and convicted of third-degree murder, the verdict was reversed, and the case was not retried. Observers suspected that one of the witnesses may have been the killer, but the authorities had zeroed in on the guilt of the man they viewed as the "bad guy."[15] This was not a case of first-degree murder, but if the dynamics of the legal authorities' "probable criminal" were operative in a first-degree murder case, the results would be even more devastating.

The question of error, like all questions pertaining to the death penalty, has two sides. Depending on the vantage point from which one views the question, the probability of error is seen as small or large. For one who regards deterrence, retribution, and the sanctity of the dead as the prime considerations, twenty-three lives sacrificed to justice is a small number, as is the figure of 139 men and women possibly mistakenly sentenced to death. On the other hand, for one who believes that deterrence is small and who rejects retribution, who views the death penalty as intrinsically immoral, even twenty-three is a staggering number, and 139 near-deaths is intolerably high.

But an even more staggering number of murderers who have been legally released under probation or parole have murdered again. For example, during the years 1985–87 an average of 290 prisoners received the sentence of death from courts throughout the United States. At year's end in 1985 and 1986, thirty-two states reported an average of 1,686 prisoners under the death sentence, all for murder. At the end of 1987, thirty-four states reported a total of 1,984 such prisoners. This gives a total average of 1,785 prisoners under sentence of death[16], of whom 11 percent had a prior homicide conviction.[17] This means that, out of this group of offenders alone, 196 innocent lives were lost as a result of the release of murderers. Extrapolating from these figures, and taking into rough account the increase in U.S. population since 1900, we may estimate that, between 1900 and 1986, at least 1,380 *additional* and unnecessary murders occurred as a result of our having released convicted murderers.[18] For retentionists, to juxtapose the twenty-three misexecuted against those inadvisedly released who have murdered again (1,380) is a greater study in horror. To both sides, such a figure points up the necessity of doing one of two things: either speedily but fairly executing first-time, first-degree murderers, or else *never*, under any circumstances whatsoever, releasing them.

10

Homicide or Suicide?

The more it is different, the more it is the same.
— Alphonse Karr

A N Oklahoma truck driver stops to have a bite in a Texas lunchroom. He is sitting peacefully on his stool when suddenly a man enters the restaurant and without word or warning kills the truck driver with a blast from his shotgun. When the police ask him why he shot the truck driver, the murderer responds, "I was just tired of living."

In late December–early January 1976–77 the American public was fascinated by the spectacle of convicted slayer Gary Gilmore fighting to die while lawyers for the American Civil Liberties Union (ACLU) and other organizations were desperately trying to stave off his execution. Gilmore had twice attempted suicide and had repeatedly stated that he wished to die by firing squad (as opposed to hanging, the other option available under Utah law). Gilmore was convicted of the July 20, 1976, slaying of a Utah motel clerk and admitted the killing of a law student working at a service station the night before.

The night of January 6, a team of Utah lawyers flew to Denver to seek to overturn a court decision to stay Gilmore's execution once more; early in the morning hours, lawyers representing agencies opposed to the death penalty were working to continue the moratorium. The state lawyers were successful in their Denver mission: the stay of execution was overturned.

Word was sent to Utah. The warden, knowing of Gilmore's wishes and weary of the on-again, off-again execution, issued the fatal "Let's do it" edict. Without waiting for news from Washington—which, it turned out, would have been negative—Gary Gilmore was led into the execution chamber and strapped to a chair; a light focused on him, enabling the firing squad of four—there were blanks in only one gun—to aim at Gilmore's heart. Within two minutes all his vital signs had ceased.

Gary Gilmore got his wish. He had wanted to die, by either suicide or execution. The state obliged.

The ACLU has several times put forth the novel idea that a condemned person does not have the civil right *not* to appeal his or her death sentence. It must have puzzled many people—if they made the connection—that the ACLU had been insisting simultaneously that the pathetic, years-comatose Karen Quinlan had a "right to die" despite the fact that she could not be consulted. What illogicality was at work there that apparently one has neither the right to live nor the right to die? Is the state disempowered to effect either course? In the Gilmore case, the state made no legal changes in the sentence that had been duly handed down; it was merely allowing matters to take their normal course, *with the permission of the accused.* In the Quinlan case, the state had set a legal precedent in permitting the removal of life-support systems, *in expectation of a proximate, resultant demise*, with the absolutely necessary proxy consent. Gilmore exercised his right to live or not to live; Quinlan exercised neither her right to live nor a right to die.

Like the Texas gunman, Gary Gilmore had grown tired of living. He was tired of living in prison, where he had spent much of his life. He had expressed his contempt for those who had wanted him to go on living by filing appeal upon appeal; he had then instructed his lawyer to cease doing so and to assist those who wanted to execute him.

Gary Gilmore, the criminal who could be sensitive and poetic, was also a cold-hearted killer who had blasted innocent people into kingdom come. He could show remorse over what he had done. But now he had but one goal: to end a life that had been burdensome, had somehow been stacked against him, and had nothing left to offer him. Enough was enough!

To discuss Gary Gilmore's desire to die as exceptional and therefore of no broad consequence to a consideration of the death penalty seems wrong and short-sighted. Since Gilmore's execution ended the near decade-long moratorium on execution, at least one other man, Jesse Bishop, also expressed the wish to die, rejected further appeals, and made his intention clear.

No, it was all not really exceptional—not the Texas gunman, nor Gilmore, nor Bishop. In 1964, H. O. Lowery, a lifer in an Oklahoma prison, addressed a formal request to a judge that he be allowed to die in the electric chair. During an escape from the prison, Lowery had engaged in several acts of violence. If one jury would not satisfy his craving for death, he said, then he would commit further acts and another jury would agree to have him killed. He had pleaded guilty to a murder charge several years earlier in the hope that he would die, but the officials had not kept their part of the bargain.[1]

There is no lack of evidence, according to Sellin's 1959 study, The Death Penalty, that the death penalty invites violence. Neither the death wish nor the violent act to fulfill it is always on the conscious level. There are cases on record of persons who confessed to murders they did not commit because somehow they wished to die. We may ask in all innocence why they didn't commit suicide; several, it seems, tried but at the last minute lost their nerve. Such nerve apparently was not needed for killing someone else and thereby achieving their goal indirectly.

It seems strange that people of frightening world-weariness, who look upon life itself as a prison, who fall into deep depression, would be afraid to kill themselves but would kill others in the hope of getting themselves killed by the state. Louis L. West and George F. Salomon report on several such cases they themselves encountered in their psychiatric practices and other case histories in the psychiatric literature.[2] The "suicide-murderers" were not always afraid of doing away with themselves the direct way; several had tried it once, twice, or more and failed pitifully in their attempts. They claimed it hurt too much, or they didn't know how to do it properly, or it was easier by the alternative road of murdering. Obviously, the choice to take this road was not always made on the conscious level. In some instances the suicide-murderers were not even clearly informed about the status of the death penalty in the state they chose for their crime; but they nonetheless seemed intent on the state's "fulfilling its part of the legal contract." For them, execution was not a threat but a promise, one they counted on and one that would finally enable them to exit from an existence that had become odious.

In these cases (which are less rare than an outsider might imagine, though no clear statistics exist), the death penalty is less a deterrent than an invitation. For all suicide-murderers—whatever the differences among them—suffered grievously as youngsters owing to impossible physical-psychological conditions in the home. There was the angry, authoritarian, brutal father drowning his failures in drink and abusing a helpless, masochistic mother who had to suppress any maternal feelings she ever had. They were parents who were often demanding but gave little in return—and what they did give was largely destructive. The seriously deviant behavior of the parents—with their drinking, beatings, and violent outbursts filling the loveless home atmosphere with terror—eventually led the hapless youngsters to seek refuge in private fantasy. As they grew older, the internal controls that restrain violent conduct in normal beings and keep behavior within acceptable bounds were gradually weakened. Then they began to descend into hell, which made suicide a half-conscious but steady craving. Murder became the means of achieving it.

Thus, some psychiatrists blame the death penalty itself for some of the murders committed in this century. As they see it, suicide-murderers have a need to be punished because they see themselves as all bad and with no real right to exist. Partaking of life means for them being enclosed and surrounded, under a bell jar from which there is no escape other than the ultimate escape.[3]

Of course, the psychodynamics described above do not have universal validity. Frederic Wertham, also a psychiatrist, reported in his 1949 *The Show of Violence* the story of Madeline, a good mother who had loved her children, but who had come to loathe herself after discovering that her husband had been mainly homosexual during their marriage. Her depression was such that it totally beclouded her judgment and made her see everything about herself as worthless and debased. Without much prior thought she engaged in what she saw as a three-way "suicide pact," in which she would do the work for her two children and then kill herself. She killed the children first; then she tried to kill herself twice, first by drinking acid and then by jumping from a second-floor balcony. Neither attempt did the trick. Instead of what she perceived as a three-way suicide, her act became a double murder and attempted suicide.[4]

Madeline had not come from a violent home. Her father had

been pleasant, but he had left the family early, undoubtedly to escape his overly serious, perhaps overly moral wife. The girl did not enjoy being sent from one parent to the other and felt closer to her mother. She had a perfectly healthy and normal brother. When she grew older, she dated men who were her social and intellectual inferiors and ultimately married such a man ten years her senior. When friends advised her not to marry him—they had heard rumors that he consorted with men—she simply could not conceive of the man as so depraved. She married him, but after a few weeks he distanced himself from her. When child number one arrived, he was pleased, but he resented child number two. He absented himself more and more. Finally, incontrovertible proof appeared that he preferred men. Madeline's subsequent psychological decomposition was internal, so that her murder of her two children took family and friends by surprise.

The psychological proximity of suicide to murder, and of murder to suicide, has been commented upon in the literature of abnormal psychology as well as in that of penology. One may not accept that capital punishment breeds murder as an axiom, but there is little doubt that capital punishment is one road to a successful suicide. Killing oneself coexists with killing others in the minds of troubled individuals as means of solving their problems.

One could hardly claim that suicides will continue only as long as the death penalty exists. But it is possible to think, with Albert Camus, that as long as the death penalty exists, wars will also exist. All three—suicide, executions, and wars—have this element in common: they are violent ways to come to terms with the individual's, society's, or the nation's frustrations and grievances, legitimate or otherwise.

In his 1966 volume *Murder Followed by Suicide*, D. West commented on the fact that in England close to half of all murders were followed by suicide attempts. One-third of these attempts were successful; thus, in a sense, one-third of the murderers executed themselves. In the Scandinavian countries, which have no death penalty statutes, nearly 40 percent of people who kill others find a way to also kill themselves. Many kill themselves out of a sense of remorse or despair at having taken another's life; still others do so to avoid the shame of accounting and punishment.

While hardly the foremost problem in the discussion of the death penalty, the relationship between murder and suicide and the relationship between the death penalty and suicide are sometimes tenuous, sometimes pronounced. Certainly, murder and suicide are both death-seeking behaviors that stem from serious pathology. The thesis bears testing that even so cold-blooded an act as accepting a contract to kill another human being—seemingly a deliberate, rational deed—has at its roots some of the same elements found in the murder of a lover, a family member, a rival, an enemy—whomever. Murder, executions, and suicides are not only death-giving but also death-seeking and (rhyme not intended) death-reeking. All three are denials of life, even if some claim that executions, in a special way, represent an affirmation of it.

11

Where Do We Stand Today?

Families of victims have neither peace nor vengeance; killers, no
certain punishment; justice, no resolution.
— *Newsweek*, May 4, 1987

O NE of retentionists' chief arguments against permanent imprisonment as the alternative to the death penalty is the cost of
maintaining these "bits of human garbage" for the remainder of their
lives, while millions of decent people have to struggle to support
themselves and their families. We hear—especially from people
versed in determining costs, of thinking in concrete dollar-and-cents
terms—the brutal fact that an execution is but a one-time expenditure, however high. Society therefore should not be asked to preserve the lives of murderers, and certainly should not make life easy
and pleasant for them.

No one can argue with this last point. But life in prison is hardly
the pleasant, carefree life that opponents of imprisonment suggest.
Perhaps those found guilty in the Watergate scandal or of insider
trading or of white-collar crime serve time in prisons that resemble
country clubs, with fences and unlocked gates. But the average penitentiary to which a lifer is consigned hardly resembles a country
club.

As for the question of costs, they are indeed high. If a twenty-
year-old prisoner is given a life term—and we mean a *life* term, not
one with parole after six to twenty years—society will be responsible
for his or her upkeep for sixty or more years. The present annual
cost of maintaining a prisoner is enormous. In 1980, extrapolating
from U.S. government figures, the lowest annual expenditure per

prisoner was that of Texas, which spent $2,241 for each adult prisoner; the highest was New Hampshire's $15,946; and the national average was $9,094. Allowing a modest 4 percent increase per year through 1988 for inflation, we arrive at a present-day annual figure of almost $12,000. Couple this cost with the per-cell construction cost of $47,500 (also calculated on the basis of the government's average 1980 figures plus 4 percent), and the grand total for care for sixty years is a mind-boggling $720,000, excluding unusual inflationary factors and the original construction expense.[1]

This awesome figure would seem to underscore the importance of preventing crime. Unfortunately, our present ability to do this seems close to zero; the mounting crime statistics and our overcrowded jails suggest that we are actually retrogressing in a serious way. Our progress in the social and human sciences has been pitiful, slower than a snail's pace, compared with progress in the physical and natural sciences. Even the suggestion that we try to remove the economic, social, and psychological causes of crime is likely to raise skeptical eyebrows. Such a goal is seen as long-range and as being more feasible in a simpler, more optimistic age than in our more cynical one. We therefore seem "stuck" with evildoers living out their lives in prison at a debilitating cost to the public.

Yet to argue that society should execute human beings in order to save money would be a frightening confession of our society's nonhuman values. Can we really place a dollar value on a fully formed life, however ill-lived? Can we conscientiously do away with a human being made in the image of God for fiscal reasons? If we are going to execute, let us execute on even the dubious grounds of deterrence, retribution, satisfying human need rather than because it costs too much to keep a human being alive. The social and moral implications of killing to reduce costs are frighteningly clear. When people reach the venerable age when their social usefulness is in question, we still provide costly and time-consuming treatments for them, expensive cancer therapies and the latest treatment in cardiac technology. Will we one day decide that the cost is too high, that the life is totally useless, that, in other words, it is too expensive for the individual to remain among his or her family, among the living?

The thought is horrifying, and our answer can only be no.

And yet the costs are high, extravagant. But ways can be found to make long-term prisoners earn their keep. They may grow what they eat by working on large prison-owned and -supervised farms in the growing season, and they may clothe themselves by making clothing in the off-season, but some mode of reducing the costs of lifelong imprisonment may be found. In an age of rising prison population, creative solutions other than furloughs and releases will have to be found.

There remains another question: what about the life-term prisoner who kills again—in prison? Isolation for several months may be an alternative; but afterwards, there may be no choice. This may well be the one situation where the death sentence is clearly and miserably indicated, necessary, with no alternatives. Admitting this justified execution does not invalidate all previous arguments against the death penalty; it is truly a choice between the lives of other prisoners and the life of the perpetrator, who cannot be wholly and for the rest of his life isolated from other prisoners. There is no conceivable alternative.

But a mandatory death sentence for killing in prison creates a new problem. An inmate may become weary of his prison existence but lack easy means of doing away with himself. He knows he will surely die at the hands of others if he kills again. For a suicide-killer, a mandatory death penalty for killing in prison would be a tantalizing opportunity, since he would have nothing—but nothing—to lose.

Another problem with mandatory death sentence for killing in prison is that conditions in prison, despite obvious differences, bear many similarities to life on the outside. It does not take much imagination to envision lawyers and protest groups quickly working to explain the innocence of the prisoner-killer or the mitigation of the circumstances. Even more cynical thinkers note the paradox of executing a prisoner-killer but punishing someone who has murdered even serially with "mere" imprisonment, sometimes for only a handful of years.

In chapter 2 the tendency in the Western world to move away from the death penalty was touched on. Certain international organizations that have a high level of prestige, such as Amnesty International, have made the abolition of the death penalty and torture two of their top priorities. Their surveys, like those of organizations exclusively concerned with abolishing the death penalty, report extensively on developments in Western countries, where capital punishment has been virtually outlawed, and in Islamic and Third World countries, where it is going strong.

From *Furman* in 1972 until the resumption of executions in 1977, the eventual elimination of capital punishment in the United States seemed to be only a matter of time. Most of the Western nations, after all, decisively abolished it. After Britain abolished the death penalty, it even gave itself the option of reintroducing it within five years, but despite a marked increase in murders, Parliament never chose to bring the hangman back. West Germany, the site of numerous terrorist acts, has abolished the death penalty (mostly because of its part in World War II) and has not seriously considered reintroducing it. Among relatively modern states elsewhere, Israel has outlawed the death penalty on the whole but reserved it for Nazi criminals who committed untold horrors on the Jewish people. Only one person, Adolf Eichmann, suffered the ultimate penalty there. None of the so-called Arab terrorists have been legally executed there, although such legislation has been under consideration. There appeared to be no good reason why the United States, with its rich history of at least somewhat altruistic programs worldwide, should not follow in the footsteps of West Germany, France, Britain, and Italy. The intellectual-cultural heritage of the Western world would seem to ensure that the death penalty would meet with growing hostility from an increasingly better educated public. Just as pressure had built up in France and Britain to exile the hangman or beheader, so sooner or later a decision by the Supreme Court—which had finally agreed to involve itself in capital punishment matters—would put an end to the death penalty. Failing that, state legislatures would remove capital punishment from their statutes, if pressure on them were maintained. There, too, the executioner would soon be looking for new employment.

But it was not to be. The forward march of the death penalty was in the end arrested in this country. Perhaps this is because, while homicide rates in the Western European democracies are increasing somewhat, there is no comparison with homicide rates in the United States. The factors are many and complex, but there is little doubt that much of Europe's increase in crime has been due to the arrival of new residents in Western Europe from Third World countries, which has created countless social problems and exacted from the host countries predictable, if often unwarranted, resentment and prejudice. The United States is even more heterogeneous in makeup—and the contents of its "melting pot" are not being covered up the way they used to be. Moreover, the drug problem in the United States has also kept rates of violent crime high. In economically prosperous Connecticut, Hartford, a core city of about 170,000, reported forty-one homicides in 1988 (below the record of forty-six set in 1980) and as many as seven in a single week in December.[2] Bridgeport, slightly larger, reported thirty-nine murders. New Haven, in the same population group, had twenty-one. Police in both Bridgeport and Hartford identified drugs as by far the leading cause for the murders; cocaine alone was a factor in 51 percent of the murders. Bridgeport attributed 95 percent of all its killings to the drug scourge, and New Haven saw 68 percent of its homicides as drug-related. None of the Bridgeport slayings were "justifiable," i.e., committed in self-defense or due to temporary insanity whereas three of the forty-one in Hartford were ruled "justifiable."

There were only twenty-four slayings in Hartford in 1987 and twenty-eight in 1986. What accounts for the recent rise? Experts claim that the use of cocaine tends to create greater violence in drug users. Wide use of cocaine also causes increased competition among sellers, and drug dealers are "more likely to settle their differences or arguments through the use of violence." Increased cash, in turn, enables the competitors to buy more sophisticated weapons. A Bridgeport police captain echoed the Hartford findings, relating the increase in murders to an increase in drug trafficking, with all its concomitant side effects.

Seven homicides were reported in New York City on the day before Christmas 1988 alone. This brought the year's total in the Big Apple to 1,842 homicides, one more than the 1987 total, which had been the previous record. Again, law enforcement agencies blamed the increase on the use of cocaine and its potent derivative, crack. In the drug-free year 1945, the total number of murders reported was a meager 291. The sixfold increase forty-three years later is terrifying and depressing. Police claim that 42 percent of all city murders can be traced back to drugs in one form or another.

This vast increase in homicides has occurred at a time when capital punishment is once again on the scene of American justice. One need not be a genius to recognize that capital punishment, as presently administered, has had few, if any, deterrent effects and has apparently not created feelings of awe toward the law; if there is a relationship between the death penalty and crime rates, it would seem to be a negative one. At most, the death penalty has helped to satisfy public anger and inner agitation, by "doing something" and getting rid of the "trashy troublemakers" that make this an uneasy country to live in. Capital punishment has somehow reassured the public, even if it has achieved nothing positive. For the emotions of the public, the landscape has been rendered a trifle less bleak.

Although drugs have now begun to invade some segments of European society, they have not yet had a comparably devastating effect in raising the homicide rate there. Whether the cry for reintroduction will be heard if the drug situation worsens remains a subject for speculation.

The Death Penalty Abroad

How was the death penalty abolished in the Western European and other nations? Let us examine their particular situations on a country-by-country basis.

In the final years of the reign of "Madame Guillotine" in France, the percentage of executions of convicted murderers was low (as indeed it has been in the United States for over two decades). Experts have attributed France's low homicide rate to the certainty of the nature of the penalty to be inflicted and *that it would be carried out speedily and efficiently.* The few atrocity murderers who were executed also had this certainty.

French public opinion polls favored the death penalty; the younger generations opposed it, but older groups clearly approved. In spite of this, the French electorate tended to select deputies for its National Assemblies who were opposed to capital punishment. In many ways, these representatives of the people saw their function as leading rather than merely reflecting public opinion.

Although both President Valéry Giscard d'Estaing and his prime minister also opposed capital punishment, their combined influence on the Assembly was insufficient to carry the day for abolition. Only in 1981, after François Mitterand's Socialist party received an overwhelming electoral mandate and formed a Popular Front government with Communists, was the death penalty abolished. The guillotine—after its career of allegedly "perfect" and "painless" executions during the French Revolution—finally became, quite literally, a museum piece.

In Britain, the hangman was long kept busy for many varied offenses. But in 1965, Queen Elizabeth II, an opponent of executions, signed an abolition bill, bringing to an end a campaign to abolish capital punishment. Sometimes the abolitionists' efforts seemed close to success; but they were throttled in that house of tradition, the House of Lords. There the older, more entrenched social groups—who had supplied few victims to the hangman in the twentieth century—felt more comfortable and secure with a death penalty statute on the books.

In spite of the efforts of the devoted abolitionists in the House of Commons and a speech by the Queen's cousin in the House of Lords, abolition was an uphill struggle all the way. In 1965, Prime Minister Harold Wilson, a Labourite, was sympathetic enough to allow members of the House of Commons to default on party discipline and vote as they saw on the issue. Parliament conscientiously set aside one morning a week for two months to consider and debate the issue until it could see its way clear to a decision. Through this intensive study, the members of Parliament arrived at their decision and "voted their conscience"—in favor of abolishing the death penalty. But in typical British fashion, a cautionary note was added: Britain was to do without capital punishment for five years and then review the results.

At first it appeared that the experiment was failing—in the year after abolition, there was a steep increase in the homicide rate. In 1965, there were only 493 murders in Britain, but there were 538 in 1966 and the following year, 570. But this result could not be regarded as conclusive since there was an equally steep increase in all crimes of violence. After 1967, the increase slowed perceptibly or even declined, in rates both of murder and of other crimes of violence.

When the time came for reconsideration in 1969, Parliament permanently did away with the hangman. Yet in 1970, following the second votes, the murder rate once again escalated perceptibly, without any apparent explanation. The highest post-abolition homicide rate was in 1972, which recorded 1,102 murders; the rate had fallen just as precipitously to 704 by 1977.[3]

Because of these mixed and even puzzling statistics, the cry for reintroducing the death penalty has been heard more loudly in Britain than in any of the continental countries. Yet each attempt has met with failure, even when it came to the highly inflammatory IRA terrorist murders in the streets of London. Not even Prime Minister Margaret Thatcher was able to reverse the vote in favor of reintroducing capital punishment.

If terrorist murders have a renewed upsurge, it is not inconceivable that British public opinion will in desperation demand the return of capital punishment. Mrs. Thatcher has warned that "vicious young people who go out and murder people . . . should not go out in the knowledge that their own lives cannot be forfeited." People's understandable anger and helplessness in the face of terrorism, with its surprise, ruthlessness, idealistic dedication, and pitiless involvement of innocent people (who might even be sympathetic to their cause if they knew what it was), may indeed open the door in Britain to a return of capital punishment for terrorists. From there, it may be only a small step to impose it for other crimes.

By now, most Britons may well have forgotten the cases that in the pre-abolition period led many to question the death penalty. One was the Evans-Christie case, in which a highly suggestible, nearly moronic truck driver, John Evans, confessed to the murder of his wife. Evans apparently confessed out of a guilty conscience, but the versions of the murder that he told differed enough that the police and courts were completely baffled. At one point, Evans implicated a neighbor, John Reginald Christie, in the murder. Christie swore he was innocent, reminding the courts of his years of stalwart service on the police force. Evans was finally convicted of murder and executed. Christie seemed to be free of suspicion when, all of a sudden, a number of bodies were discovered in his yard and residence, to all intents and purposes revealing him as a mass murderer. It became evident to nearly all that Christie had committed the crime for which Evans had been executed. A fair-minded Britain was shocked, and a bill to abolish the death penalty that one member had introduced year after year got a more respectful hearing.[4]

A report by the chief investigator who had been designated by the home secretary was assailed in the press as an attempted whitewash and an effort to compound the judicial crime by justifying Evans's execution. Those striving to end capital punishment, led by the indefatigable M.P. Samuel Sydney Silverman (the head of the chief organization for overall penal reform) and segments of the press, remained convinced that Evans had been wrongfully convicted.

Two other cases involving executions which, for one reason or another, were highly questionable in regard to verdict and execution had taken place previously. They too cast doubt on the fairness of the judicial system and its ability to differentiate adequately between degrees of severity of a crime. This kept the debate alive in the postwar decades, a debate that Britons should be wary of forgetting under the present pressures of terrorism.

The constitution adopted by the Federal Republic of Germany in 1949 specifically provided against the use of the death penalty. The "new Germans" were mindful that Hitler's regime, which had brought them shame and suffering, had considered only the rights of the state and had totally ignored those of the individual. More than those of other nations, the postwar German social and legal thinkers saw capital punishment as a human rights issue. The right to live, which Nazism had violated several million times, now became a sacred right that no state, no judge, and no other authority could even consider violating.

Between 1882 and the end of World War I, the highest number of death sentences imposed in Germany in a single year had been forty-seven, which—coincidentally—is also the average for Germany over those same years; of those sentenced to death, the average number executed was seventeen, or 36 percent. More political murders of distinguished Germans took place in the five years following World War I: the number of people sentenced to death rose to 89 in 1919 (36 executions), 113 in 1920 (36 executions), 149 in 1921 (28 executions), 124 in 1922 (26 executions), 77 in 1923 (15 executions), and 112 in 1924 (23 executions), or an average of 111 sentences and 23 executions.[5] The dynamics of political justice in those years is too intricate to discuss here, but it is interesting to compare the use of the death penalty in these years with the number of executions under the early Nazi regime—an average of 95 sentences and 106 executions between 1933 and 1939. In the three years immediately preceding the outbreak of war, the number of executions markedly exceeded the number of death sentences imposed by the politicized courts.[6] There were numerous arbitrary killings by the state through its secret police, the Gestapo, and by the SS, the political-military arm of the Nazi party. Life had become terribly cheap. The doctrine of the supremacy of the state and the good of the party and society created a new, arbitrary rationale for killings not ordered by the traditional law-enforcement agencies. (In the USSR, under the dictatorship of Josef Stalin, the number of state-ordered executions also exceeded the number of death sentences. It is clear that dictators use their alleged certainty of what is good for the state and party to deal with their enemies. Dictators on both the Right or Left have shown a common disdain for the life and the humanity of the individual.)

Since their resurrection from the rubble heap that was Germany in 1945, the Germans have bent over backward to respect the dignity of man and the importance of human rights. They did so when they outlawed the death penalty. In all discussions since—no matter which party was in power—Germans have adamantly insisted upon the continued abolition of the death penalty. The many recent terrorist attacks, using violence for political goals, on leading Germans and selected foreign groups have caused voices for reintroduction to be raised. Their arguments for reintroduction have been the same as in all countries: the restoration of justice, the safety of society, retribution, deterrence, and the lower cost than life imprisonment. Yet not only have these attempts been rebuffed, but Justice Minister Hans Engelhard has taken the lead in insisting that abolition become a part of the West European Declaration of Human Rights.[7]

Japan, like Germany, had a prewar reputation for law-enforcement harshness. Its prewar police force had been vested with great authority, authority that was frequently abused. Since World War II, Japan has been intent on changing this image, and its police have shown great restraint in capturing terrorists, willful murderers, and others who have used violence. Japan has retained the death penalty, but it uses it sparingly: the offense has to be "directly dangerous to human life" (e.g., willful murder or sabotage of transportation resulting in death), imperil the community (e.g., setting fires in residential quarters), or be political (insurrection or inciting aggression), all of which endanger general safety. All in all, seventeen specifically enumerated crimes could lead until recently to capital punishment.[8] Recent revisions in the penal code have reduced the number of crimes that may lead to the ultimate penalty.

Proponents of the death penalty find it consonant with Japanese culture, values and traditions, but occasional attempts have been made to eliminate it. Compared to the United States, however, Japan scarcely has a problem at all. There is far less crime, fewer persons are sentenced for capital crimes, and fewer than three persons are executed in any given year.

The death penalty is deeply entrenched in the Third World countries of Africa and Asia, in the Moslem nations, and in isolated pockets of the democratic industrialized countries. Like earlier stages of development of many Western countries, the slowly developing nations of Africa and Asia have more pressing things to do than concern themselves with unfamiliar, "advanced" notions of justice. Moreover, some are ruled by dictators all too eager to frighten the population into a state of acceptance by making summary executions (without sentencing) often as common as death penalties imposed.

The Moslem world is also still modernizing. In fact, the resistance of the partisans of tradition to modernization, both between and within countries, is largely responsible for the present ferment in the Middle East and especially their people's hatred of the United States. The nation in that region that has executed more "enemies" than any other is Iran, whose former ruler, the shah, sought to modernize the nation and in the process garnered the hatred of traditionalists among the mullahs. The United States, with its emphasis on the individual, on the relativism of values, and on the human sciences (which were often in conflict with Islam), became "the devil." To the mullahs and their young followers, everything American was the embodiment of evil.

To retain the superiority of Islamic culture and law, the regime of the Ayatollah Khomeini carried out executions as rarely before. Some of the capital crimes were political, as when someone evinced an unwillingness to see the truth of revolutionary dogma. The crime could be sexual, when deviation from Islamic law occurred. Amnesty International, which is as well informed as any agency, has called these executions cruel, inhuman, and degrading and has stated that the political and religious prisoners—perhaps the same people—received ultrashort trials that were merely pretexts for dispatching them to the next world. In its *Law and Human Rights in the Islamic Republic of Iran*, Amnesty International draws a gloomy picture of justice under the mullahs, which has led to far more tortures and executions than the shah's regime ever provoked.[9]

The death penalty has survived almost uniformly in Moslem countries perhaps because of the relative rigidity of Islamic law. Secular authorities, where and when they have intervened in judicial administration, are still influenced by the indissoluble bond of religion and law in Islam—a bond not readily evident or comprehensible to the Western observer. For example, adultery, which means any sexual relationship outside of marriage (especially for the woman), remains among the most serious of crimes, as does apostasy, i.e., abandoning Islam as a religion.

Islamic law on the subject of murder may strike the modern Western eye as either very advanced or very backward. It builds on the older notion of vengeance but gives vengeance a legal structure. The family of the victim and the state divide the responsibility for achieving justice. It is the responsibility of the state to consider the evidence and to determine the guilt or innocence of the accused; the state may also determine what type of punishment is applicable. But carrying out the sentence is left to the family of the murder victim. The family may commute the court's sentence; for example, if the sentence is death, it may be commuted to blood money, or—in an unlikely case—the penalty may be dropped altogether. But the family may not exceed the sentence of the court; a sentence of blood money cannot be changed by the family into a death sentence.

The fact that the nations most like the United States in cultural, social, and religious background have outlawed capital punishment is not cause for us to follow suit. We have problems that are beginning to plague them only now. The influx here of many immigrants—some uprooted, many poor, just as many desperate and lost—and the innumerable problems of race and ethnocentrism have fostered a drug culture that was until relatively recently of only minor consequence. Perhaps if other countries experience a significant rise in crime accompanying the drug evil they may be led to once again dole out death sentences. Yet even if some do reinstitute capital punishment, it would still be wise for us to examine the foreign experience. After all, the British Royal Commissions that have considered the dilemma of capital punishment have seen fit to go abroad and inquire about the various impacts of abolition and retention. Surely the example of Britain can inspire some of our wavering states to do with or do without capital punishment for a limited period of time and see what the effect would be under controlled conditions.

We can also study the many countries that do execute, either in large numbers or only rarely and symbolically. Do they have good cause for what they are doing? How is our experience different from theirs, and our backgrounds and aspirations? Is there merit in the Islamic system of having the family of the victim play a part in carrying out a sentence?

Clearly, our cultural distance from other societies enables us to view them more dispassionately and with better perspective. There is surely no harm in looking across borders and oceans, for while aspects of the use of the death penalty derive from particularities of cultures, just as many are universal.

A Word in Closing

We have tried diligently to present both sides of an issue of great moral, social, and political import. We hope that this balanced approach has given rise to sober reflection so that the reader will have facts and trends clearly in mind if a decision of consequence is made in the near future. We have shied from expressing our personal views except where, as any reasonable person might, we have hinted at our outrage over injustices committed in the name of justice, whether they served the cause of abolitionists or retentionists. The very complexity of the question; the continuing increase in crime generally; the absence of a sense of shame in evildoers; and frustration at trying to serve both humanity as a whole and the victim in particular have, we recognize, rendered U.S. state and federal governments impotent in providing a clear-cut solution. The time may have come to admit this and to fish or cut bait, lest we continue to drift along in indecision. Time and again, proponents and opponents have argued the matter of deterrence, the religious issues, the historical angle, the practical side, and humane ways of dealing with the death penalty. Is there no other approach?

There is no assurance that capital punishment as presently practiced deters people from murder; nor does the abolition of the death penalty substantially increase the incidence of capital crimes. Yet there is also no real proof of the deterrent effect of life imprisonment. The religions of the world, and even the divisions within a given religion, are often uncertain, ambivalent, and at cross-purposes over the matter. History should teach us something; but *what*? Whenever a step in one direction has been taken, succeeding years and different circumstances have caused a reaction in the opposite direction. Practical considerations have all too often appeared crass, unfeeling. The humane approach is ambiguous; as Dostoyevsky said, "He who sympathizes with the criminal can never sympathize with the victim." But as Shakespeare wrote in *All's Well That Ends Well*, "The web of our life is of a mingled yarn, good and ill together: our virtues would be proud if our faults whipped them not; and our crimes would despair if they were not cherished by our own virtues."

Is there no unequivocal stance to assume, no way out of this binary opposition of opinions? Maybe not, maybe so. What if we took what we have and made a decision one way or the other? What if we were to demonstrate more reliably the deterrent effect of the death penalty and resolutely executed those convicted, reheard past all reasonable appeal? On the other hand, what if we rewrote our laws such that we had no capital crimes on the books? What if we commuted the sentences of all those now on death row to life imprisonment? What if we eliminated plea bargaining? Such questions could continue.

But one major, inescapable fact remains: the United States has already essentially given up the death penalty. The number of convicts sentenced to death has continuously decreased; the number of those actually executed is a mere trickle of what it used to be, far fewer than the number of people on death rows or sentenced to long prison terms. Criminals know this; law-abiding citizens know this. If the American people are not willing to see that the laws requiring execution are carried out fairly and speedily in the name of justice, then they should be willing to abandon those laws. It is hypocritical to straddle the fence; it is clear from the facts presented that it is moral to come off the fence on either side.

Even apart from moral arguments, the system is amiss. It is slow and lacking in efficiency, and it costs taxpayers a bundle to mount countless appeals by court-appointed attorneys year after year. It is cruel—yes cruel, even to the cruelest of criminals—to keep people on death row interminably, for even if hope is kept alive, it is at the expense of dire emotional upset. The state of Florida has the dubious distinction of harboring the largest number of death-row inhabitants of any state in the nation—nearly three hundred—and yet it has executed only two persons since 1986. California has almost as many on its death row and, according to several studies (including one prepared for the federal judiciary), is spending in excess of $2 million a year on appeals. Nationwide, the figure is a frightening $30 million. For those who would argue that nothing of consequence is calculated in less than billions today, we invite them to wait only a few years. The death-row population (now over two thousand) is growing at a rate of more than three hundred a year and executions are increasing by 3 percent; nonnegligent killings exceed twenty thousand each year. At this rate, we will double the number of death-row residents by 1999. Justice William Brennan maintains that capital punishment can succeed only if it is "invariably and swiftly imposed," and former justice Lewis Powell is of the opinion that we should "take a serious look at whether retention of a punishment that is not being enforced is in the public interest." It has become obvious that as a nation we are not committed to the death penalty, even though we give strong lip service to its symbolic representation. In all of 1988, we executed only eight persons. In January 1989 Theodore Robert Bundy was finally electrocuted after a decade on Florida's death row. He was convicted of the killing of a twelve-year-old girl, but he later confessed to the murder of many other young women and departed this life under suspicion of having raped and murdered dozens of others. If we truly believe in the death penalty for all right reasons—reasons of justice, morality, and social good—we should insist it be enforced under the banner of the best of American law. If we do not have the courage of our stated convictions, we should drop the charade and abolish the death penalty altogether.

Epilogue

C APITAL punishment is a life-and-death matter. The inherent dichotomy demands a balanced presentation of the subject, for the life under consideration in each case is both that of the victim and that of the perpetrator.

We came to write this book as two individuals whose perspective and sense of balance have been honed fine by many years of teaching experience in the humanities. We have discovered that the details of foreign language learning and the presentation of literature have frequently impinged upon historical, cultural, and social issues of national and worldwide import. The death penalty is an issue of past, current, and continuing relevance and one that has forced us to look back in time, at policies in various countries, and at ourselves in 20th-century America. After all , the preservation of life and its corollary, the avoidance of death, head the list of issues facing humankind at any time.

The preservation of life is not only an individual concern based on instinct but also an idealistic notion rooted in love of one's fellow human beings and grounded in theology or personal ethics. Capital punishment, of which control over life is a part, is a legal matter that serves not just the rights of individuals but the rights of the state for the protection of all. Seen in an even broader context, there are implications for harmony between societies and nations and for the preservation of peace and the avoidance of war. A study of attitudes toward capital punishment can reveal much about the nature of humankind. Given "the facts," most people will react clearly one way or the other—that is, they will be for or against the death penalty. Ambivalence sets in as knowledge increases.

We have approached the topic as persons who have traveled widely and regularly over a lifetime and who have resided outside the United States. Our careers have been quite similar over many years, but we came to college teaching from different directions. One of us had his beginnings in pre-medical studies, long military service, a stint in the mortuary business, and several years in criminal and intelligence work in the United States and overseas. The other emigrated in 1935 from the Saar region as a refugee escaping Hitler's policies of political and racial murder, served in the War Department as a translator, became involved with others who were dying as political refugees, and later took an interest in capital punishment because his son had been a student of one of the foremost abolitionists.

As the reader might conclude from the sketches above, we stand on opposite sides of the fence. However, we straddle the fence together when peripheral matters muddy the waters. And we recognize that our respective positions are largely theoretical, namely, that very few persons are actually executed, and very few persons actually serve a full life sentence in lieu of execution.

For many reasons, we think capital punishment is one of the most important issues of our time.

Notes

Chapter 2

1. Jan Gorecki, *Capital Punishment: Criminal Law and Social Evolution* (New York: Columbia University Press, 1983), 45–47.
2. Ibid., 48–49.
3. Ibid., 52–53.
4. Leon Radzinowicz, *A History of English Criminal Law and Its Administration from 1750*, vol. 1, London: 1948, 24.
5. Ibid., 10.
6. Walter Berns, *For Capital Punishment: Crime and the Morality of the Death Penalty* (New York: Basic Books, 1979), 131.

Chapter 3

1. Berns, 44–50.
2. Ibid.
3. Barry Nakell and Kenneth A. Hardy, *The Arbitrariness of the Death Penalty* (Philadelphia: Temple University Press, 1987), 22–26.
4. In *Coleman v. Balkcom*, reported in *New York Times*, Apr. 2, 1981, D-23.

Chapter 4

1. Eugene B. Block, *When Men Play God* (San Francisco: Cragmont Publications, 1983), 18.
2. Quoted in Charles L. Black, Jr., *Capital Punishment: The Inevitability of Caprice and Mistake*, 2d ed., augmented (New York: W. W. Norton & Co., 1981), 44.
3. Raoul Berger, *Death Penalties: The Supreme Court's Obstacle Course* (Cambridge and London: Harvard University Press, 1982), 139.
4. Quoted in Hugo Adam Bedau and Chester M. Pierce, eds., *Capital Punishment in the United States* (New York: AMS Press, 1976), 99.
5. Gorecki, *Capital Punishment*, 26. There is always a sentence hearing following a criminal trial. The only difference in a death penalty case is that the defendant can opt for a jury (rather than a judge) to hear the evidence relevant to sentencing and decide the penalty.

6. 428 U.S. 153 (1976).
7. 438 U.S. at 586.
8. 438 U.S. at 587.
9. Mark A. Siegel, Donna R. Plesser, and Nancy R. Jacobs, eds., *Capital Punishment*, Information Series on Current Topics (Plano, Tex.: Information Aids, 1986), 13.

Chapter 5

1. Stephen Nathanson, *An Eye for an Eye?* (Totowa, N.J.: Rowman and Littlefield, 1987), 27.
2. Thorsten Sellin, *Capital Punishment* (New York: Harper & Row), 122–124 and 239–253.
3. Ernest van den Haag and John P. Conrad, *The Death Penalty: A Debate* (New York and London: Plenum Press, 1983), 143.
4. Block, *When Men Play God*, 46.
5. Bedau and Pierce, *Capital Punishment*, 249.
6. Quoted in Block, *When Men Play God*, 46.
7. Ibid.
8. Ibid., Royal Commission on Capital Punishment, 1949–53.
9. Hugo Adam Bedau, "Deterrence and the Death Penalty: A Reconsideration," *Journal of Criminal Law, Criminology and Police Science* 61 (1970):546.
10. Van den Haag and Conrad, *Death Penalty*, 65.
11. *Fowler v. North Carolina*, Supreme Court of the U.S. #73-7031, Brief for the U.S. as amicus curiae, 36.
12. Isaac Ehrlich, "The Deterrent Effect of Capital Punishment," *American Economic Review* 65 (June 1975): 398.
13. Berns, *For Capital Punishment*, 102.
14. Koestler, *Reflections on Hanging*, 13.
15. Gary E. McCuen and R. A. Baumgart, *Reviving the Death Penalty* (Hudson, Wis.: Gem Publications, 1985), 85.
16. Ibid., 60.
17. Quoted in Block, *When Men Play God*, 51.
18. Van den Haag and Conrad, *Death Penalty*, 69.
19. *Parliamentary Debates*, House of Lords, May 30, 1810.

Chapter 6

1. Quoted in Ramsey Clark, "The Death Penalty and Reverence for Life," in *The Death Penalty*, edited by Irwin Isenberg (New York: H. W. Wilson Co., 1977), vol. 49, no. 2, 119.
2. Rabbah B. Abbuha, *Talmud: Sanhedrin*, 52A.
3. Benjamin Cardozo, *Law and Literature* (New York: Harcourt Brace, 1931), 93f.
4. Clark, "The Death Penalty," 12.

Chapter 7

1. 408 U.S. at 450.
2. Ramsey Clark, *Crime in America* (New York: Simon and Schuster, 1970), 335.
3. 408 U.S. 238; Bedau and Pierce, *Capital Punishment*, 196–200.
4. Cited in McCuen and Baumgart, *Reviving*, 78.
5. *Capital Punishment: A National Prisoner Statistics Report, 1982*, U.S. Department of Justice, Bureau of Justice Statistics (Washington, D.C., 1984).
6. Even the casual observer will notice many distinct changes for the better in the South since 1954 and a considerable worsening of conditions for blacks elsewhere, particularly in the urban industrial communities of the Northeast, where there are strikingly more examples of prejudice.
7. Quoted in McCuen and Baumgart, *Reviving*, 73.
8. Quoted in ibid.
9. Ibid., 74.
10. William J. Bowers and Glenn L. Pierce, "The Illusion of Deterrence in Isaac Ehrlich's Research on Capital Punishment," *Yale Law Journal* 85 (Dec. 1975): 187–208.
11. Ibid.
12. The authors are not aware of studies of reactions to blacks killing non-whites and non-blacks.
13. Berger, *Death Penalties*, 54, and Hans Zeisel, "Race Bias in the Administration of the Death Penalty: The Florida Experience," *Harvard Law Review* 95 (1981): 456.

Chapter 8

1. Quoted in Bedau and Pierce, *Capital Punishment*, 127, 206.
2. 408 U.S. at 413.
3. 408 U.S. at 390 (Burger, C. J., dissenting).
4. "Moral Judgments about Capital Punishment: A Developmental-Psychological View," Lawrence Kohlberg and Donald Elfenbein, in Bedau and Pierce, *Capital Punishment in the United States*, 247f.

Chapter 9

1. McCuen and Baumgart, *Reviving*, 97.
2. Ibid.
3. Statement in the French Chamber of Deputies, August 1930, quoted in *Report of the Select Committee on Capital Punishment, 1929–30*, ¶222. But many claim the statement is apocryphal or attribute it to Thomas Jefferson, who is alleged to have said, "I shall ask for the abolition of the punishment of death, until I have the infallibility of human judgment demonstrated to me."
4. Clark, *Crime in America*, 335.

5. Hugo Adam Bedau and Michael L. Radelet, "Miscarriages of Justice in Potentially Capital Cases," *Stanford Law Review,* 40 (Nov. 1987): 33, 70, 47, 56.
6. Ursula Bentele, "The Death Penalty in Georgia: Still Arbitrary," *Washington University Law Quarterly* 62 (1985): 597–600.
7. *Hartford Courant,* Nov. 30, 1988.
8. Ibid.
9. Quoted in Black, *Capital Punishment,* 43.
10. ABA report commented upon in *Hartford Courant,* Dec. 1, 1988.
11. Bedau and Radelet, "Miscarriages," 60f.
12. John Guinther, "The Kindness of Strangers," *Welcomat* (Philadelphia, Penn.), November 14, 1988.
13. Ibid., and Bedau and Radelet, "Miscarriages," 156 (David Wayne Robertson).
14. Guinther.
15. Ibid.
16. U.S. Department of Justice, *Bureau of Justice Statistics Bulletin: Capital Punishment for Years 1985, 1986, 1987,* 1.
17. U.S. Department of Justice, *Report to the Nation on Crime and Justice,* Bureau of Justice Statistics, 2d ed., 99.
18. *Statistical Abstract of the United States,* 107th ed., 1987, 8. (This figure is based on an average population of 104 million between the years 1900 and 1940 [100 received under death sentence on average × 11% recidivism × 40 years = 440]; 163 million between 1940 and 1965 [150 × 11% × 25 years = 412]; 218 million between 1965 and 1986 [200 × 11% × 24 years = 528]).

Chapter 10

1. Louis Lolyon West, "Psychiatric Reflections on the Death Penalty," in Bedau and Pierce, *Capital Punishment,* 426.
2. Ibid., 419–31, and George F. Solomon, "Capital Punishment as Suicide and as Murder," in Bedau and Pierce, *Capital Punishment,* West 432–44.
3. West, 433.
4. Frederic Wertham, *The Show of Violence* (New York: Doubleday, 1949), 26f.

Chapter 11

1. Joan Mullen, Kenneth Carlson, and Bradford Smith, *America's Prisons and Jails,* vol. 1, *Summary and Policy Implications of a National Study* (Washington: U.S. Government Printing Office, 1980), 67, 119.
2. Connecticut material in this section is from *Hartford Courant,* Dec. 26, 1988.
3. Block, *When Men Play God,* 144.
4. Ibid., 149f.
5. *Der grosse Brockhaus,* 18. Auflage, Grundgesetz Kommentar, edited by I. von Münch, Art. 102, 573.
6. Ibid.

7. Statement by government spokesman Friedhelm Ost at a press conference in Bonn, Oct. 14, 1987.
8. McCuen and Baumgart, *Reviving*, 112.
9. Cited in ibid., 123f. Also, "Iran, the Death Penalty," Amnesty International, AI Index: MDE 13/06/89, Jan. 1989.

Nakell, Barry, and Kenneth A. Hardy. *The Arbitrariness of the Death Penalty*. Philadelphia: Temple University Press, 1987.

Shapiro, Martin. *Law and Politics in the Supreme Court*. New York: Free Press of Glencoe, 1964.

Siegel, Mark A., Donna R. Plesser, and Nancy R. Jacobs, eds. *Capital Punishment: Cruel and Unusual?* Information Series on Current Topics. Plano, Tex.: Information Aids, 1986.

White, Welsh S. *The Death Penalty in the Eighties*. Ann Arbor: University of Michigan Press, 1987.

Wolfe, Burton H. *Pile-Up on Death Row*. Garden City, N.Y.: Doubleday, 1973.

Wright, Charles. *Federal Courts*. St. Paul, Minn.: West Company, 1963.

Zimring, Franklin E., and Gordon Hawkins. *Capital Punishment and the American Agenda*. Cambridge: Cambridge University Press, 1986.

Bibliography

Bedau, Hugo A. *The Courts, The Constitution, and Capital Punishment*. Lexington, Mass.: Lexington Books, 1977.
———. *The Death Penalty in America*, rev. ed. Garden City, N.Y.: Doubleday Anchor Books, 1967.
Berger, Raoul. *Death Penalties: The Supreme Court's Obstacle Course*. Cambridge and London: Harvard University Press, 1982.
Berns, Walter. *For Capital Punishment: Crime and the Morality of the Death Penalty*. New York: Basic Books, 1979.
Black, Charles L., Jr. *Capital Punishment: The Inevitability of Caprice and Mistake*. New York: Norton, 1974.
Block, Eugene B. *When Men Play God*. San Francisco: Cragmont Publications, 1983.
Clark, Ramsey. *Crime in America*. New York: Simon and Schuster, 1970.
Cox, Archibald. *The Role of the Supreme Court in American Government*. New York: Oxford University Press, 1976.
Davis, Bertha. *Instead of Prison*. New York: Franklin Watts, 1986.
Draper, Thomas, ed. *Capital Punishment*. vol. 57. New York: H. W. Wilson, 1985.
Freund, Paul A. *On Law and Justice*. Cambridge, Mass.: Belknap Press of Harvard University Press, 1968.
Gettinger, Stephen H. *Sentenced to Die*. New York: Macmillan, 1979.
Gorecki, Jan. *Capital Punishment*. New York: Columbia University Press, 1983.
Van den Haag, Ernest, and John P. Conrad. *The Death Penalty: A Debate*. New York and London: Plenum Press, 1983.
Von Hirsch, Andrew. *Doing Justice*. New York: Hill and Wang, 1976.
Isenberg, Irwin. *The Death Penalty*. New York: H. W. Wilson Co., 1977.
Jackson, Bruce, and Diane Christian. *Death Row*. Boston: Beacon Press, 1980.
Levy, Barbara. *Legacy of Death*. Englewood Cliffs, N.J.: Prentice-Hall, 1973.
Levy, Leonard W. *Against the Law: The Nixon Court and Criminal Justice*. New York: Harper and Row, 1974.
Loeb, Robert H., Jr. *Crime and Capital Punishment*. New York: Franklin Watts, 1978.
Lowell, Robert. *History*. New York: Farrar, Straus and Giroux, 1967–1973.
McCafferty, James A., ed. *Capital Punishment*. New York: Aldine, Atherton, 1972.
McCuen, Gary E., and R. A. Baumgart. *Reviving the Death Penalty*. Hudson, Wis.: Gem Publications, 1985.
Moore, Mark H., Susan R. Estrich, Daniel McGillis, and William Spelman. *Dangerous Offenders*. Cambridge and London: Harvard University Press, 1984.

Nakell, Barry, and Kenneth A. Hardy. *The Arbitrariness of the Death Penalty.* Philadelphia: Temple University Press, 1987.

Shapiro, Martin. *Law and Politics in the Supreme Court.* New York: Free Press of Glencoe, 1964.

Siegel, Mark A., Donna R. Plesser, and Nancy R. Jacobs, eds. *Capital Punishment: Cruel and Unusual?* Information Series on Current Topics. Plano, Tex.: Information Aids, 1986.

White, Welsh S. *The Death Penalty in the Eighties.* Ann Arbor: University of Michigan Press, 1987.

Wolfe, Burton H. *Pile-Up on Death Row.* Garden City, N.Y.: Doubleday, 1973.

Wright, Charles. *Federal Courts.* St. Paul, Minn.: West Company, 1963.

Zimring, Franklin E., and Gordon Hawkins. *Capital Punishment and the American Agenda.* Cambridge: Cambridge University Press, 1986.

Index

About the Authors

DONALD D. HOOK has been a professor at Trinity College since 1961. He is the author of several trade books and textbooks and has contributed many articles on linguistic and social questions in such journals and newspapers as *The Anglican Theological Review, The Journal of Popular Culture, Anglican and Episcopal History, International Review of Applied Linguistics, The Hartford Courant*, and pedagogical journals here and abroad.

LOTHAR KAHN was professor emeritus of Central Connecticut State University, where he taught from 1946 to 1987. He was the author of two volumes on modern French and German literature and several trade books and textbooks. He had contributed articles and essays on social and cultural questions in such journals and newspapers as *New Leader, Midstream, Christian Century, Christian Science Monitor, The Hartford Courant*, and many Jewish journals here and abroad. Professor Kahn died in January, 1990.